MISBEHAVING

'Deeds not Words'
Albert Hall, London, 20 November 1970: Photo by Leonard Burt © Getty

MISBEHAVING

STORIES OF PROTEST AGAINST THE MISS WORLD CONTEST AND THE BEAUTY INDUSTRY

Edited by

Sue Finch
Jenny Fortune
Jane Grant
Jo Robinson
Sarah Wilson

The Misbehavers

(Sue Finch, Jenny Fortune, Jane Grant, Jo Robinson and Sarah Wilson)

in association with

The Merlin Press Ltd.

Central Books Building, 50 Freshwater Road, Chadwell Heath, London, England RM8 1RX

merlinpress.co.uk

Photo facing title page by Leonard Burt/Central Press used by permission of Getty Images

Photos from the film *Misbehaviour* used with permission of Pathé UK

ISBN 9780850367676

Printed in the United Kingdom by Imprint Digital, Exeter

First Edition

Designed and typeset by Morgan Stetler

CONTENTS

I was not at the event as I'd only

arrived in London three weeks before.

However, I recall reading the slim

pamphlet about the event and the

trial, as soon as it appeared, and

I'd say it was the first thing that

really turned me on to feminism,

so moving and exciting,

and of course, I never looked back.

—Lynne Segal

WOMEN'S LIBERATION AT FIFTY — A BIG THANK YOU

I wasn't at the first UK Women's Liberation Movement conference at Ruskin College in 1970 or at the protest against the Miss World contest of the same year.

But I want to pay tribute to those women who were, and who made those things happen, at a time when UK patriarchy was still red in tooth and claw.

Married men had a legal right to rape their wives. There were no domestic violence refuges or rape crisis centres. Many employers openly advertised job vacancies as being for men only. Sometimes, even if a job was open to women, the ad would specify that she must be 'attractive'.

If a woman found that she was being paid less than a man doing the same job for the same employer, she had no legal redress.

Maternity leave was not a legal right. Neither was state-funded childcare. Women seeking a mortgage or other credit were often required to provide a male guarantor.

Most married women were not allowed to fill in their own income tax returns: they had to give their financial information to their husbands, who would fill in the forms on the couple's behalf. Husbands, by contrast, were not required to reveal their financial information to their wives.

Many social security benefits for couples and families were only payable to the 'head of household', i.e. the husband.

Contraception was not available on the NHS. In some areas, help was available from clinics run by charities or local authorities, but some of these would only help women who were married or engaged.

I could go on, but those of you who are old enough will remember life before Women's Liberation, and those of you who don't remember will probably have heard.

All of the above examples of institutional sexism (and many others) have now been abolished or at least reformed.

This is due, in large part, to the energy, commitment and activism of the Women's Liberation activists who decided to change the world in 1970.

To them I say a big thank you.

—Zoë Fairbairns

Introduction

Misbehaving marks the fiftieth anniversary of one of the key years in feminist history: the disruption of the 1970 Miss World contest by a dramatic action that contributed to the growth of the Women's Liberation Movement in the UK.

Some of the writers infiltrated the Miss World contest at the Royal Albert Hall in London, which was then one of the main highlights of the TV calendar: *'in a matter of hours, a global audience had witnessed the patriarchy driven from the stage'*. (British Council, 2 May 2019) We threw leaflets, flour, smoke and stink bombs, bringing the show and live TV transmission to 100 million people across the world to a standstill. This witty, noisy but peaceful *coup de theatre* together with the women's actions at the trial, were key events that brought a radical new movement, the Women's Liberation Movement, into every home in the country.

Misbehaving includes stories by some of the women who took part in the Miss World protest, as well as women who felt its impact, and about the trial of women arrested during the protest. The book was compiled by a collective of five women who took part. Two of us were arrested and tried for offences related to the Miss World protest. We put out a call for contributions from women who were at – or impacted by – Miss World 1970, and these are woven into and between our stories. We asked two of the contestants (the winner and runner-up) to contribute their views too, but they chose not to.

The book aimed to coincide with the release of a film about the event, *Misbehaviour*. We met with the writer, director and producer of the film during the long road to making it, to discuss our involvement in the protest and the early women's movement. Their stories about why they wanted to make the film are included in *Misbehaving*, along with a contribution from the presenter of the Reunion radio programme that sparked their interest, and the maker of a BBC documentary about the Miss World protest, *Beauty Queens and Bedlam*.

Linking the Miss World protest in 1970 to the struggle of women for the vote fifty years earlier, *Misbehaving* moves on to a critique of the beauty industry now, fifty years later, and the continuing struggles of women across the world against sexual abuse, rape, violence against women, racism, economic inequality and sexism.

Sue Finch, Jenny Fortune, Jane Grant, Jo Robinson, Sarah Wilson

Sue Finch ONE OF THE PROTESTERS AGAINST THE MISS WORLD CONTEST IN 1970

Our slogan for the Miss World protest was 'We're not beautiful, we're not ugly, we're angry!' But why were we so angry?

We came from a generation of angry women. My mum left school at sixteen and joined the navy. Leaving Hull for the first time, she was stationed in Malta during the war, and remembered it as the best time in her life. She met my Dad in Malta on her twenty first birthday, married him two weeks later, and had three children in quick succession when she came back to live in London. Like many women after the war she didn't work out of the home again – and often said how hard it had been to have three children under four, no washing machine, no friends or family near. Many women were pushed back into the home after the war, when the 1500 wartime nurseries that had provided childcare for over 71,000 children were closed.

It was even harder for her after my older sister died when I was eleven, my brother was ten, and our family fell apart. The year after, I ended up in a relationship with a man twice my age. It was only when my daughters turned twelve that I could see it must have been closer to abuse than a relationship. I was lucky though, I got to a grammar school that had been founded by a strong supporter of universal suffrage and was the first person in my family to go to University.

Then it was 1968 and Martin Luther King was shot. Students and workers were rioting in Paris in May. Revolution was everywhere. I answered an ad in a newspaper for an international student work camp in Cuba. It was incredible, an eye-opener. We stayed in huge tents surrounded by mango trees and sugar cane and went in trucks early every morning to dig holes with pickaxes and plant coffee before it got too hot. In the evenings, Cuban activists came and talked to us about how the revolution had been won in just six years, how hard life had been before 1959 and how women had played a major role in overthrowing the old corrupt system. Cuban women talked to us about the 'Revolution within the Revolution', their struggle for women's equality. We went to hear Fidel Castro give a speech (for hours!) saying that although the social and economic systems in Cuba had been transformed by the revolution, social relations had not changed enough – yet. As the camp went on, fewer and fewer of the 600 international students turned up for the early morning coffee planting – and those that did were mostly women. I got to meet Jane and Sarah there, and we became friends, meeting up again at a women's conference in 1970, starting a women's group, moving into a commune together then demonstrating against the Miss World contest.

By February 1970 I was wondering what I was doing with my life, just pregnant but didn't know it, and working in a petrol station when I heard about a Women's Liberation Conference in Oxford. I went, and it was amazing. There were powerful women talking about the politics of the family, housework, bringing up children, women in trade unions, equal pay...all together for the first time. There was a great crèche, run by men, and Morgan, my partner's three-year-old son, loved it. For the first time I understood that politics included all of us, women and children too.

The co-ordinating committee set up by the conference came up with four demands: equal pay, equal education and job opportunities, free contraception and abortion on demand and free 24-hour nurseries. The Equal Pay Act

The crèche, Women's Liberation Conference, Ruskin College, Oxford, February 1970: Photo © Sally Fraser

was passed later in 1970, and came into force in 1975, but almost fifty years later women still earn 16% less than men, and most women end up clustered in low paid work. More progress has been made with equal education (only 7% of women went to university in 1970, now slightly more women than men go in England). There's free contraception and abortion in England, but not in many other countries. Some free early education has been fought for and won (I was never sure about the demand for 24-hour nurseries from the child's point of view!), but the quality is variable.

Jane and Sarah were at the women's conference too and we wanted to keep talking, so began to meet as a women's group in each other's flats. The London Women's Liberation Workshop had started up in 1969, and there seemed to be women's groups everywhere. Different groups wrote different issues of a newsletter, Shrew. My partner went back to live in America, and I ended up moving into a commune in Islington set up by Sarah, Jane and others from the women's group, seven months pregnant and with my partner's son.

The women in the commune talked and talked and read books about women's liberation; *Sisterhood is Powerful*, an American anthology edited by Robin Morgan, had a great effect on us. We wanted to be recognised for who we were. The more we talked into the night at our women's group, the more we felt that what really held us back, and kept us powerless, was being judged by — and then judging ourselves by — how we looked.

When Sarah went to a meeting where the Peckham Women's Liberation Group suggested a demonstration against the exploitation of women at the Miss World competition at the Albert Hall in November 1970, we all wanted to do it. The Miss World contest seemed to us the most exaggerated example of women being judged like cattle. The contest had been compulsory viewing in my house when I was growing up, and in most houses that had televisions. But as far back as I could remember it had made me angry, the way women were paraded, made to turn around, and judged by their looks and 'vital statistics' (usually 34-21-34). We wanted to make a public statement that it was not acceptable any longer – and to bring the contest to an end.

Protests against beauty contests had started in the USA in 1968, and there had been a small demonstration against Miss World in London in 1969. We met to plan the next Miss World demonstration at our commune in October 1970 and put together a leaflet calling the event a degrading cattle market. We were clear that the protest was not against the contestants, but against Mecca, the organisation that made money out of them. All I can remember of that meeting is lying on my back on the floor, like a beached whale, and coming up with the slogan, 'We're not beautiful, we're not ugly, we're angry!'

Someone bought tickets and on the night we all went separately into the Albert Hall. My seat turned out to be at the very top, so nine months pregnant and carrying flour bombs and leaflets tied above my bump under a huge old brown coat I heaved myself up endless stairs and sat through what felt like hours of contestants being paraded.

Bob Hope, the 'Master of Ceremonies', was on stage on his own making sexist jokes when Sarah gave her football rattle signal to start and I tipped bags of flour and leaflets over the balustrade. They floated down like snow. After that, it was chaos. A surprising number of other women let off joke stink and smoke bombs and blew whistles, the whole hall seemed to be filled with falling flour and smoke and leaflets. Bob Hope dived for the floor.

I was thrown out down the endless flights of stairs by two bouncers and found myself hoping this might bring on labour as I was already overdue. But when they realised how heavily pregnant I was they just put me out on the street and didn't arrest me. There was a great demonstration going on outside as well, with placards saying *Mis-fortune demands equal pay for women, Mis-conception demands free abortion for all women, Mis-placed demands a place outside the home*. Everything had been organised by word of mouth; there were

THE COMPETITION WILL SOON BE OVER

.....WE HAVE BEEN IN THE MISS WORLD CONTEST ALL OUR LIVES......

JUDGING OURSELVES AS THE JUDGES JUDGE US - LIVING TO PLEASE MEN -

DIVIDING OTHER WOMEN UP INTO SAFE FRIENDS AND ATTRACTIVE RIVALS -

GRADED, DEGRADED, HUMILIATED...........WE'VE SEEN THROUGH IT.

MECCA ARE SUPERPIMPS SELLING WOMEN'S BODIES TO FRUSTRATED VOYEURS UNTIL

AGEING BUSINESSMEN JUMP YOUNG GIRLS IN DARK ALLEYS - BUT THEY'RE ONLY

SMALL-TIME PIMPS IN OUR EVERYDAY PROSTITUTION: WOMEN'S BODIES USED BY

BUSINESSMEN TO SELL THEIR GARBAGE - LEGS SELLING STOCKINGS, CORSETS

SELLING WAISTS, CUNTS SELLING DEODARANTS, MARY QUANT SELLING SEX......OUR

SEXUALITY HAS BEEN TAKEN AWAY FROM US, TURNED INTO MONEY FOR SOMEONE ELSE,

THEN RETURNED DEADENED BY ANXIETY.

WOMEN WATCHING.................................WHY ARE YOU HERE?

THE MAN'S MAKING MONEY OUT OF US WE'RE NOT BEAUTIFUL OR UGLY WE'RE ANGRY

no mobile phones then, and no phone at the commune —so it was a complete and wonderful surprise that there were so many people there.

Exhilarated but exhausted, I got the bus home. We found out later that about 100 women had protested inside the Albert Hall, many more people had demonstrated outside, and five women had been arrested for assault, offensive weapons (a child's smoke bomb) and abusive language. My daughter Kelly was born ten days later, and I gave her the surname 'Wild': I wanted her to have her own name – not my father's or her father's – and grow up to be independent.

The Miss World action was the first feminist event since the women's suffrage movement to generate mass publicity in the UK. It was also the first conspicuous act of civil disobedience on behalf of the British women's movement since the suffragettes. (Coote and Campbell, *Sweet Freedom*, 1982) The demonstration made headline news and broke new ground in getting live TV coverage. Miss World was broadcast live on TV to 30 million viewers in the UK, and over 100 million worldwide. The *Daily Mirror*, under a front-page headline 'MISS WORLD! AND OH, WHAT A WILD, WILD WORLD', quoted Bob Hope saying:

> I want to tell you, anyone who would break up an affair as wonderful as this, they got to be on some kind of dope
> *Daily Mirror*, 21 November 1970

The *Guardian* repeated the same quote:

> Anyone who would break up such a wonderful affair, wonderful people, wonderful girls has got to be on some kind of dope, believe you me. Sooner or later these kind of people have got to be paid off. There's someone upstairs sees to it. God, of course, being a man. *Guardian*, 21 November 1970

The trial of the five women arrested took place at Bow Street Magistrates court in February 1971, and Jenny and Jo decided to defend themselves. Over fifty years before, the suffragettes had used their trials to make public statements and eventually won the vote for women; they were our heroines. Women eventually won the vote by 'deeds not words', but fifty years later in 1970 only 4% of MPs were women. Another fifty years on, and over 100 years since some women got the vote in the UK, still fewer than a third of MPs are women.

Jenny and Jo were wonderful in court—calling the judge 'Daddy', challenging his patriarchal authority and power 'YOU are the representative of a legal system which exists to defend property, which depends on a family structure which oppresses women' Jenny said. Jo was pregnant and got re-arrested and held overnight for trying to go to the toilet, and I was arrested for trying to stop the police jumping on her and was held overnight. At that point I was incredibly grateful that everyone in the commune looked after the children.

Supporters demonstrated outside the court each day for five days with banners saying 'Miss Trial', and 'End Sexploitation' but it didn't get much good publicity. One of the best was Anne Sharpley's report in the *Evening Standard* (11 February 1971):

> Militant women back in the dock at Bow Street;
> the first since the Suffragettes.
>
> Could it really be starting up again?
>
> Could anyone have guessed in 1905 when the patrician Emmeline Pankhurst and the mill girl Annie Kenny opted for going to prison instead of paying their fine that it was the start of nearly a decade of fury and fighting?
>
> Is this the start of another such decade?

Katherine Whitehorn commented in the *Observer*:

> The fact that everyone is talking about them would seem to justify louder antics, like disrupting the Miss World contest; but it's unfortunate to this extent, that anyone who doesn't want to take them seriously can too easily write

them off as a set of furies who will not rest till the last
husband is strangled with the guts of the last psychologist,
and sperm flows in the rivers down the gutters of Park
Lane. And this they are not. Who are they? Not, actually, a
set of horsehair lesbians, as advertised.

Observer 14 February 1971: 'Women's Lib – Could it Happen Here?'

The *Daily Mail* 21 November 1970 printed a picture of Miss World and a demonstrator with a headline which read: 'The Beauty and the Bovver Girl'. The *Daily Express* ran the headline: 'Miss World Uproar ...with a moo moo here and a protest there... Stink bombs greet Bob Hope in demo then Miss Grenada wins title'.

We had organised the protest so quickly that we hadn't had time to think about how to get good publicity. Most of us saw the media as being biased and male dominated and thought the chance of fair reporting was small. So we decided to write a Women's Newspaper (which only survived three issues), and then a pamphlet 'Why

L to R: Jo, Sue, Sarah and Jenny working on the first issue of the Women's Newspaper in the Women's Liberation Workshop Office, Little Newport Street, London, 1971: Photo © Sally Fraser.

Miss World?' about the action and the trial, complete with great cartoons by Jenny and Jo. We researched more about the profits and corporate power of Mecca at Companies House, learning slowly that research and publicity are key to successful actions.

On March 6th 1971 we all went on the first International Women's Day march in London – in the snow. Many women carried placards saying 'We're not beautiful, we're not ugly, we're angry!' Some women were pulled along in cages labelled 'Mis-stress', 'Mis-Fortune' and more, while others carried symbols of women's oppression (rubber gloves and aprons).

Thousands of women danced and sang along Oxford Street (an ironic version of a 1930s song):

Symbols of Oppression,
Women's march,
8 March 1970:
Keystone Pictures
USA/ZUMA Press

> Keep young and beautiful
> It's your duty to be beautiful
> Keep young and beautiful
> If you want to be loved.

Since I'd arrived at the commune pregnant, and with a three-year-old, and found that there were no nursery places – or only places for children considered to be at risk of coming to harm, I hadn't been able to work. So I had been claiming benefits, in those days the 'Unsupported Mother's Allowance', as my contribution to the food kitty. The allowance had to be claimed from the post office weekly and could be stopped immediately if a man was seen to be staying over – as men were supposed to be financially responsible for mothers. Jo, Jenny and I had been so angry about the treatment of women at the benefits office that we had set up a local branch of the Claimants Union, with others, to support women who were being cut off benefits because a man had stayed over, or evicted because they couldn't pay their rent. We wrote an *Unsupported Mothers Handbook* to make sure women knew their rights, with more great cartoons by Jo and Jenny.

The Claimants Union led straight to squatting, as so many women and children were being evicted because they couldn't pay the rent, and there were so many empty houses. We became good at 'opening up' houses for people who needed them, and borrowing trucks to help them move in. Eventually four of us left the commune and went squatting in a Housing Association house that had been empty for years. We got taken to court for eviction. However, we had found evidence that all the Directors of the Housing Association were also being paid as Surveyors and Builders, against charity law; Jenny brought this up in court, and the *Guardian* printed a big article about it. We won our appeal to the High Court and all got rehoused; the Housing Association was taken over by another charity.

We had started a creche for our own children in the commune (by that time there were three, after Jo's baby Sam Wild was born in May 1971) and some of those living in our street. I loved it. As the children got older and we were squatting we took them to a playgroup in Centreprise community centre near Dalston, and I went on a course to learn more about early education. When the playgroup got evicted, we wrote to the Greater London Council (GLC) Women's Committee to ask if we could have an empty house to set up a community nursery. They asked for evidence that it was needed, so we went door to door round Broadway Market in Hackney (then a derelict area full of empty houses due for redevelopment and squats) with a survey asking women what they wanted. Two thirds of the women wanted somewhere for children to play and learn, so that they could work. We sent the findings to Hackney Council and the GLC.

One of the women who was squatting in the area got the development plans from the GLC so that we could see which empty houses would be there the longest before redevelopment. They gave us an empty house and garden, then together with a couple of women I had met on a playgroup course, we lobbied Hackney Council for funding to set up a community-run nursery, the Market nursery. After we demonstrated on the Hackney Town Hall steps and got the support of the local paper, the *Hackney Gazette*, the Council gave us some funding and we opened the nursery.

I worked there for about five years, and it is still going today – as a community nursery run by parents. It's open from 8-6 instead of 24 hours, and only free part-time for two to four year olds, but I think this still counts as part of delivering the childcare demand that came out of the women's conference in 1970. Many other community nurseries were started up by women around the same time, including five in Hackney and an earlier one that we learned from in Dartmouth Park Hill.

After that I got an early years qualification, co-ordinated a workplace nursery set up by trade unions in central London, then opened a new nursery for Hackney Council – the Mary Wollstonecraft Children's Centre. I went on to work for children's charities, and at the Department for Education for a while, and now work part-time co-ordinating an Early Years Hub funded by the Greater London Authority. The other days I play with my fantastic grandchildren.

I chose to work in early education, but also continued to campaign for women's rights and peace. Soon after my second daughter,

Two women resting (Elspeth & Margaret), and Women for Life on Earth banner, lining up to leave Hungerford on the road from RAF Welford to Newbury. 4 September 1981: Drawing © Sarah Wilson.

Leni Wild, was born in 1981, a Women's Peace camp started up at Greenham Common, and we began to go to demonstrations there and to camp for weekends with one of the Hackney Greenham Common women's peace groups.

We cut down the fence, invaded and encircled the base (30,000 women 'embraced the base' in 1983), decorated it with photos and rainbow webs, but didn't manage to stop the US Cruise missiles landing. However, we eventually succeeded in getting rid of those nuclear weapons (with some help from international peace negotiations!). The last missile left the base in 1992 and the area has been returned to 'common land'.

Now I'm part of Women in Black, an international women's peace network, still taking direct action. We blockaded Faslane in Scotland where the UK's four Trident nuclear submarines are still kept, with one always on patrol, and Aldermaston and Burghfield Atomic Weapons Establishments (where the nuclear warheads are assembled), and lay down in the road locked on to concrete blocks to stop access to the site. It took police four hours to drill us out... in the snow.

The Miss World demonstration was the first feminist protest I was involved in, and it was great that it was seen by 30 million people in the UK and over 100 million worldwide on live television. It was also fun.

Miss Grenada won Miss World that year, only the second black woman ever to do so, and went on to become an ambassador for Grenada. Pearl Jansen, the runner up, was the first black woman to represent South Africa following protests from the anti-apartheid movement.

When the Miss World contest came back to London in 2011 we demonstrated again with Feminist Network, Feminista, Reclaim the Night and Million Women Rise outside Earls Court, with signs saying Miss-Ogyny and 'being a woman is not a competition'. There are new generations of young women who are active feminists – including my two wonderful daughters – and UK feminist conferences have thousands of participants. The #MeToo and Time's Up movements of women against sexual harassment and rape have taken off.

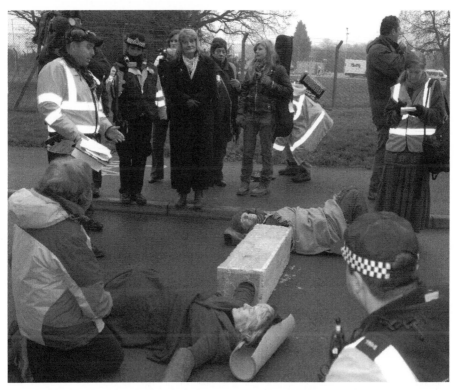

Liz Kahn and Sue Finch locked onto concrete to block road at Burghfield Atomic Weapons Establishment Photo © Cynthia Cockburn

But I'm angry that we still need to campaign, and about the two women who are killed by their partners each week in England, the many more women who live in fear, and the widespread violence against women, in peace and war. I'm angry that so many women's lives are ruined by Female Genital Mutilation. There is a continuum between women being judged by their looks, seen as objects – or cattle – and rape and violence against women.

I'm angry that the Miss World competition still carries on, since 1951 when it was started by Eric Morley. It carries on in spite of the fact that 1500 people were arrested for protesting when the contest was held in India in 1996. Or that more than 200 people were killed, 1200 hospitalised and 12000 made homeless in riots when the organisers tried to hold it in Nigeria in 2002 (it was moved to London).

I'm even angrier that Donald Trump co-owned and hosted Miss Universe, the American version of Miss World, from 1996-2005, and used his beauty pageant to boost business interests abroad. He was instrumental in getting the 2013 contest hosted by Russia, and the contacts he made in Moscow may also have helped give him the Presidency.

A hundred years after creative direct action – 'propaganda by deed' – won votes for some women, only 32% of MPs are women in the UK. Fifty years after we protested against the Miss World competition, just 1.5% of rape cases reported to the police in England and Wales result in suspects being summonsed or charged, (Owen Bowcott and Caelinn Barr, analysis of Home Office statistics, *Guardian* 27 July 2019), and only 7.5% of charges result in a conviction; 80% don't even get to prosecution. (Liz Kelly, Professor of Sexualised Violence at London Metropolitan University, quoted in the *Guardian* 13 October 2016.) And the Miss World contest carries on. So the reasons we were angry haven't gone away.

What's changed since 1970? Not enough!

Val Charlton ARTIST AND SPECIAL EFFECTS MODEL-MAKER IN FEATURE FILMS WHO DEMONSTRATED OUTSIDE THE MISS WORLD PROTEST IN 1970, AND THE TRIAL THAT FOLLOWED

I was simply awed by the bravery and insight of those women who challenged that ridiculous Miss World competition and scared the pants off Bob Hope. I always regretted that I wasn't brave enough to join them inside. Their powerful and imaginative demonstration against the Miss World competition inside the Albert Hall had a massive impact on me. Somebody phoned me on the night, and I went down to the Albert Hall but I didn't go in. I remember standing outside with a lot of other women and making a lot of noise. It was amazing!

I demonstrated outside the court on several days and followed the trial and I was so happy when they were freed.

I don't think anyone had really questioned Miss World before. It was considered normal to parade young women in bathing suits and scrutinise their bodies to 'judge' who was the most 'beautiful'. The demonstration was crucial to expose the sexism that affected all of us. Today more than ever, so many young women are incapacitated by believing that their bodies are not 'perfect' if they don't match some manufactured image with a marketing agenda. It's shocking and humiliating when the truth is that we are all unique and distinct from one another at any age – something to celebrate.

I was born in 1941, the eldest of three kids born in Sunderland, a shipbuilding town in the North of England which was badly bombed during the last war. My grandpa, Bob Charlton, was a pattern-maker by trade with his own small business supplying wooden patterns for engineering parts to the ship building industry. My father, born in 1915, left school at fourteen to become apprenticed to his father.

My mother, the eldest of four, grew up in a council house on the Ford Estate in Sunderland which housed mainly shipbuilding workers and their families. Her father, my other grandpa, was a metal worker at the Sunderland forge, beating out hot metal for parts for ships. He had been badly gassed in the First World War.

By 1946 my grandpa, exhausted by the war, decided to sell up and buy a cafe with a petrol station for £700 on the Great North Road in Yorkshire. He and my nana moved the whole family, including my dad's sister and her husband, sixty miles south to run a new business in catering, which my father knew nothing about and hated.

I was five and went to the local school three miles away in the small town of Boroughbridge. My school mates were the children of farmers and farm labourers and local villagers. My brother and sister and I grew up with a lot of freedom during the summer months because our parents were so busy that they rarely knew where we were. But all of us, when old enough, either waited on tables in the cafe or served petrol at the pumps. I lived there until my early twenties.

I failed the 11 plus exam along with most kids from our school but was transferred to Grammar School when I was thirteen because of one teacher's intervention and for reasons I never understood. That opportunity changed my life. I loved being there, though I now believe such a selective system is inappropriate. I only learned recently that because more girls than boys were passing the eleven plus exam it was government policy to mark girls lower than boys. I was furious because so many of my girl-friends with the same abilities as me were affected.

King James's Grammar School in Knaresborough was a very liberal school. Our headmistress was a lesbian living openly with her partner in a house with a swimming pool, which was fairly exotic for Knaresborough in the fifties. I was an average pupil interested in most subjects but mainly in art. After leaving school I spent a year working as a trainee window dresser at Schofields department store in Leeds. But I soon decided that if I didn't want to be a window dresser for the rest of my life, I'd better go to art school.

I was at Harrogate School of Art for five years, had a wonderful time and made friends for life. We did a lot of life drawing and painting. I took the sculpture course which included stone carving and clay modelling from life, I also studied ceramics and graphic design. There was a sense of optimism and I was unaware of any limitations on my aspirations.

I came to London in 1965 to go to London University's Institute of Education for a teaching certificate and there I met Julian, my partner for the next fourteen years and father of our two children. He introduced me to class politics. In 1966 everybody was talking about black power, the peace movement, all manner of politics, pop art, Beatles music, Mary Quant fashion; I hadn't yet discovered feminism.

In London on March 17th 1968 there was a huge anti-Vietnam war demonstration outside the American Embassy in Grosvenor Square. Two hundred people were arrested, including Julian and me. After being pushed to the front of the crowd where things had got out of control, I found myself dragged out from under a police horse and hauled into a police bus. We were all taken to Paddington Police Station and kept in a large room for hours. We were released at 2.00 am to find our way back to Camden. Soon afterwards I discovered I was pregnant.

In November 1969, when my son was a year old, I was still in shock after a very difficult childbirth. I was twenty-eight and we were living in my flat in Mornington Crescent. Until this point I had no concept of being deprived because of my gender, but I was totally unrealistic about the impact that having a child would have on my life. I loved my baby and I had wanted him very much, but I was lonely, confused and felt very inadequate in my new circumstances.

I heard about a Women's Liberation Group that had just started in Tufnell Park so I went along to one of their early meetings. It was only the second group to be set up in London; the first was in Peckham Rye. I was completely daunted by the women I met there. They were educated, politically aware, beautiful, stylish – and to my naive eye, middle-class and confident. I went to the meetings for about six weeks but then left because I didn't understand what women's liberation was about, they already seemed so liberated.

I got involved with some local mothers and we started Camden Women's Action Group to campaign for nurseries. That seemed more practical and related to my needs. We met regularly but found we were talking more and more about feminism and Women's Liberation. In 1970 we all went to the first Women's Liberation Conference at Ruskin College in Oxford and that changed everything. I remember the excitement listening to all these powerful articulate women – Juliet Mitchell and many other wonderful speakers and with men doing the crèche. Suddenly I began to click, this is important, I've got to understand what's going on, it's about raising *my* consciousness.

Early in January 1971 it was decided to organise a Women's Liberation demonstration to celebrate International Women's Day. I was very involved in a joint committee of all the different groups which was formed to organise a march through central London on the 6th of March. But then on 20th of January there was a national postage strike with no knowing how long it would last. We gave leaflets and posters for distribution to anyone who was travelling out of London but there was little feed-back and we had no idea how many women had heard about the march.

I built a giant shoe with a poem on a banner written by Sheila

Rowbotham about the old woman who lived in a shoe and had so many children she didn't know what to do. We hired a lorry to carry it as a float on the demonstration.

The 6th March was a foul day, it was snowing heavily and we could barely see out of the windows. We were all crammed into the front of that lorry driving from Kilburn up the Bayswater Road towards Speakers Corner with absolutely no idea how many people had even heard about the demonstration, let alone turned up. But as we turned into the park we saw thousands and thousands of women... and some men, with every kind of banner, placard and costume – street theatre members were singing and dancing all waiting to start the march with more women flooding in every minute. Unbelievably ten thousand women had turned up. I get shivers to this day whenever I remember that moment.

By 1972 I was working in the collective of a socialist feminist magazine called *Red Rag*. Over nine years fifteen issues were produced by a fluctuating collective of feminists, with many more contributing articles. I was mainly involved in doing layout, graphic design and cartoons. (*A digitised version of all the issues has been produced and will be available this year 2020*).

In 1973 Sue Crockford, a feminist film maker, myself and some other mothers, started the Children's Community Centre at 123 Dartmouth Park Hill in Camden, a nursery staffed by parents with funding for two full-time workers. I was involved in that project for about five years.

From 1974 until 1995 I worked on seventeen popular feature films and several smaller films as a special effects model-maker and creature costume supervisor. Nine of these were written and directed (or co-directed) by members of the Monty Python team. In January 1990 I was offered a Senior Lectureship in the Theatre Department at Wimbledon College of Art on a newly validated undergraduate course called *Technical Arts in Special Effects*. I saw an opportunity on two levels, training for film special effects and a different way of educating.

I was very committed to a student-centred approach rather than a subject-centred approach. The success of our course and high achievements of our students, where frequently, 40% of them were dyslexic, forever convinced me that when anyone is fully supported and allowed to discover where their passions lie, they are unstoppable in their learning and in their creativity.

I retired in 2009 from teaching and since then I've been writing.

'The Scales of Justice' © Val Charlton, **Red Rag** Issue No. 2, January 1973.

Sue Crockford (1943-2019) DIRECTED AND PRODUCED THE FIRST DOCUMENTARY ABOUT THE WOMEN'S LIBERATION MOVEMENT IN THE UK, *A WOMAN'S PLACE* (1971). SHE WENT ON TO PRODUCE NEARLY FIFTY DOCUMENTARIES AND SHORT FILMS AS A FEMINIST CAMPAIGNER AND COMMUNITY ACTIVIST, AND HELPED TO SHAPE CHANNEL 4's DISABILITY AND CHILDREN'S PROGRAMMING.

I came from a working-class family in Surrey and went to a girls' grammar school. When I was a girl, I was Robin Hood and Maid Marion. But when I told my headmistress I wanted to be a film director she said, 'Come down to earth, girl!'

Then I went on to Leeds University to do Art and English and was the first person to do film for my special subject, a thesis on Ingmar Bergman (they thought art was only painting). Luckily my Professor was Quentin Bell, Virginia Woolf's nephew. Someone showed me a picture of the Sharpeville Massacre in South Africa, and I couldn't believe it – it was like losing my virginity. So I started an anti-apartheid group, and put up a photographic exhibition – two people threatened to break my arms, but it stayed up.

When I came to London, I joined the Vietnam Solidarity Campaign – I've just been sent redacted information about someone who was a spy for the police in our group! I've never joined a political party until recently, when I joined the Labour party, on the grounds that 'If I can't dance, I don't want to be part of your revolution! A revolution without dancing is not a revolution worth having' (Emma Goldman).

At first, I was worried that women's liberation wasn't important enough, we should be organising around Vietnam. The women's movement was coming closer and closer to home. Instead of changing the lives of others, I thought, 'why should we always be on the outside of things?' We lived next door to a Canadian woman who was a feminist working in theatre. We became friends; we didn't have a telly so in those days you found out everything from friends.

I hadn't really experienced inequality until my son was born, then I saw a cartoon in Shrew of a man walking out of the door carrying a placard, leaving his wife behind looking after the children and knew how she felt. The women's movement became the core of everything. I joined the Tufnell Park/Belsize Park women's group in 1969 – and we are still meeting weekly fifty years later.

I heard a lot about the Miss World protest, and loved it – such visual fun, it got up people's noses. It had a huge impact. There isn't a Miss World contest for blokes, being judged by just what you look like, is there?

I saw pictures of the protest in the papers – like putting headscarves on statues, an image is worth a lot of words! I filmed the Oxford women's conference in 1970, then the first

International Day Women's march in 1971 for my film 'A Woman's Place'. Many of the women on the march carried banners or were in cages on floats saying 'Mis-represented',

Sue Crockford with Barny and Juliet Mitchell, Women's Liberation Conference, Ruskin College, Oxford, February 1970. Photo © Sally Fraser

'Mis-fortune' etc. which came from the Miss World demonstration.

After that, I set up Liberation Films, we made films and distributed US films, showing them with group discussions. When we showed Mai Zetterling's *The Girls* we asked the women who saw it if they had ever been molested or abused, and half said they had. We used film to provoke discussion.

Once the police walked in when we were about to show a film and asked if we had a certificate – I said 'no'. Then he asked if we were selling coffee and suggested that we sell the sugar lumps too so that people could see the film without paying – and he stayed to watch the film!

I helped to set up a children's community centre – 123 Dartmouth Park Hill – and made a film about it to show how we did it and encourage other parents to set up their own centres. We ran it ourselves – Camden Council gave us a house on a six-month lease, and the nursery stayed there for seventeen years. My son went, and I worked full time.

Later I ran a youth centre in Somerstown for fourteen years. I still see some of the kids – one of them said to me 'The thing that you did, Sue, was listen to us.' I made short films for deaf children, set up housing for homeless girls, and started a gay teenage group – forty-five years ago. I also made films for Channel 4, and we funded and distributed our own films.

I made a film about Mary Wollstonecraft (*Mary Wollstonecraft, the rights of man, the wrongs of women*), and filmed some of it in the Mary Wollstonecraft Children's Centre in Hackney. Feminism is like Brighton Rock, right through everything we do – it affects absolutely everything. Judge me by my son and daughter!

Before I was ill, I used to go to Women in Black vigils at the statue of Edith Cavell in St Martin's Lane. Across the top there is a quote from her: 'Patriotism is not enough. I must have no hatred or bitterness for anyone'. I wrote a script for a film about Edith Cavell. Now I'm part of the London Socialist Film Co-op – we show films every month. The next films are the *Women's Peace Crusade in 1916-18* and *These Dangerous Women* commemorating the 100th anniversary of the Women's International Peace Congress at the Hague in 1915, when 1300 women from twelve countries called for peace and mediation, then and in the future.

Sarah Wilson GREW UP
IN SRI LANKA, HITCHED AROUND
EUROPE, STUDIED ART IN
ENGLAND AND PARIS, HAS HAD
EXHIBITIONS IN LONDON AND
FRANCE. DISCOVERED POLITICS
IN ALGERIA, RETURNED TO PARIS
IN EARLY 1968, WENT TO CUBA
THAT SUMMER. LATER MOVED
TO FRANCE.

As we entered the Albert Hall that night, planning to disrupt the
Miss World contest live on air, we knew that if we succeeded our
action would be seen by a massive audience. But we didn't realise
just how big that audience would be. Over the years we came across
women who said, 'seeing that was what brought me to the Women's
Liberation Movement'; or later, 'that was what my mother said made
her into a feminist'. We met people who remembered seeing it on
TV as children, watching with their parents, not only in the UK but
across the world, as far away as Australia. It has been taught in
schools and universities as part of gender studies programmes.

The Miss World Contest was one of the most prestigious spectacles
in the annual calendar of televised events. It was dreamed up in
1951 for the Festival of Britain, by Eric Morley, who was working for
Mecca and was later to become Mecca's chairman. The pageant
was an enormous money spinner – all based on judging women by

their looks, and the shape and size of their bodies. Their so-called 'vital statistics' – their breasts, waists and buttocks. There were fifty eight contestants, from the USA, Central and South America, the West Indies, Africa, Asia, the Far East and the Middle East, and Europe, including, for the first time, Yugoslavia, part of the communist block. Judges included such eminences as the High Commissioner of Malaysia, the Premier of Grenada, the Maharaja of Baroda and, the Ambassador of Indonesia, together with figures from the world of entertainment such as the actress Joan Collins, the singer Glen Campbell, and Nina, of the Nina and Frederik singing duo.

Presiding over them all as chairman was Peter Dimmock, the general manager of BBC Outside Broadcasting. We learned later that there was a big brouhaha about the winner of the Miss World crown that year. She was Jennifer Hosten, of Grenada and one of the judges was the Premier of Grenada. The bookies favourite, by far, had been Miss Sweden. Jennifer was only the second black woman to win the prize, and Miss Africa South, also black, came second. Sectors of the population became very exercised about this, and some of the audience themselves protested outside the Albert Hall afterwards, shouting 'Swe-den Swe-den'. I wonder whether they stood next to the feminist protestors, and the Gay Liberation Front and the Young Liberals demonstrating against

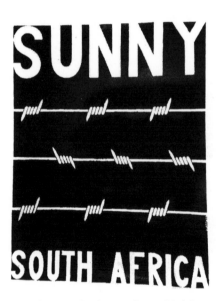

Anti-apartheid poster: Poster Workshop

Apartheid. That would make for a heady mix. Julia Morley, who was the organising director, resigned four days afterwards because of pressure from the newspapers. However, after her husband, Eric

'Groping my way out of a fog of unawareness at the first Women's Conference at Ruskin College'.
Photo © Sally Fraser.

Morley, published the judging panel's results she returned to her job, and when he died in 2000 she took over the chair.

The guest presenter, flown over from the US, was the veteran American comedian, Bob Hope. He was there to entertain the audience with his jokes. At Christmas he would take the winner of the Miss World contest to Vietnam to provide light relief for the GIs there, as he had done in previous years.

What led to this?

In early 1970 I and some other women friends had been to Britain's first Women's Liberation conference. This was held in Ruskin College, Oxford. It was a landmark in what became known as the second wave of feminism and women's liberation in the UK – the first wave being the Suffragette movement, demanding the vote for women, at the beginning of the 1900s.

Today it is hard to imagine the power of the impact of this two-day event, attended by 600 women activists. It was organised entirely by women, with only women speakers, and an agenda based on

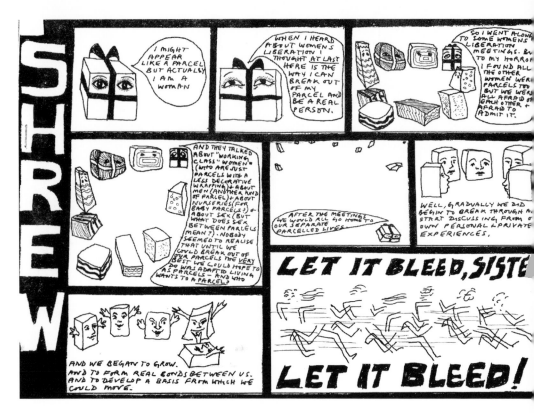

women's issues. Only fifty women had been expected, so clearly there was a huge desire to address these issues. There were a few men in the audience, and there was a creche run by men, partners of the women organisers. Even having a creche on the premises was new. Women were expected to make other arrangements for the care of their children, or more often, at mixed gender events they would be left 'holding the babies'.

None of us had ever experienced anything like this before. This was to be a watershed in my life, in the lives of many of us. It was the first time I had been to a political event which was entirely about women. I find it hard to remember now how very different that felt, and how empowering it was. This was about our own lives. Until now our struggles had been very much about justice for other people: civil rights, liberation, anti-racism, anti the Vietnam war movements, support for industrial action, decent wages, housing and work conditions. But all those actions were with men, who, in one way or another, tended to dominate and take centre stage. Whilst resenting the restrictions and patronising attitudes of the society we'd grown up in, I, at least, had not felt I had a case to make on my own behalf. I had slowly been groping my way out of a fog of unawareness, but I had barely begun.

On our return to London we set up a small consciousness raising group, as did many other groups of women in London and elsewhere. We met up once a week in each other's houses, and shared experiences of our lives growing up as women; our relations to our families, to men, our hopes and fears about jobs and careers, society's expectations of us, our feelings about our bodies and sexuality. We found that the way we related to each other was different when men were not present. Those discussions transformed the way we experienced the world and our relation to it. The slogan 'The Personal is Political' was one of the most powerful and expressive slogans of that time. And whilst there was relief and joy and laughter which flowed from these discussions, there was also anger at what women had been, and were still being, subjected to.

Clearly, though, discussions in small groups were not enough. There was also a desire to do something, for action, to protest against the injustice women experienced, and to make the world a fairer place. We also came to appreciate that where things were better for females, in the long run they improved for men: 'Liberate women and you'll liberate men'.

In September 1970, at the end of a women's conference in London Jan Williams and Hazel Twort stood up and announced that the annual Miss World contest would be held at the Royal Albert Hall in November and proposed a demonstration against it. Anyone interested in joining them was invited to a meeting. Jan and Hazel were from the Peckham Women's Group. They both had small children and had met at the Peckham Rye One O'clock club, a community centre where pre-school children and their parents could gather to socialise and play. Hazel had presented a paper at the Ruskin Conference about Women and the Family, which she, Jan and another woman had written. The Miss World contest had become a major event in the annual TV calendar. I can't remember how much of this I had watched in the past, when still at home with my parents; I suspect they might have thought it was a bit 'beneath them'. But then there was nothing else to watch on the night of the contest, there were only two channels in those days, and it was such a big spectacle the other channel didn't even try to compete. I certainly had an idea of what it was like, the long parade of women in swimsuits

Planting trees and coffee on terraces in Cuba, 1968.
Photo courtesy of Chris Allen.

showing off their tits and bums, having to walk and swirl around, and push their breasts forwards, arching their backs the better to display their bottoms, and finally being judged on the shape and statistics of those bodies. All this in front of an audience themselves in full evening dress and televised live to millions of people in the UK and across the world. A massive money spinner for Mecca, the owners of the contest. I thought it was a wonderful idea to demonstrate against that. It was so huge, so very public, so exploitative of women.

There were only five of us at this first meeting. We were disappointed, but still felt we could have an impact. We decided to buy five tickets in 'the gods', high up above the stage, both because they were the cheapest, but also because it was a good place from which to throw things down. Leaflets, especially, would flutter conspicuously down through the air, like autumn leaves. I suggested we hold the next meeting in the house where I lived in north London. It was a large household, where there were always lots of people coming and going. It was likely to boost our numbers – which it did. People in the street often referred to it as a commune, a description which we didn't like very much, but it stuck. Although it was a mixed household, none of these planning meetings included men. The idea for the house had evolved out of our women's group, and included Jane Grant, Sue Finch, Sarah Martin and me. Later Jo Robinson joined us there, as did Jenny Fortune.

Jane, Sue and I had met in Cuba in the summer of 1968, on a camp of international volunteers, planting coffee and trees in Pinar del Rio. There had been drama even before we left for Cuba. The events of May '68 in France threw the Western governments into a panic. Many countries banned the flights to Havana. The authorities believed we were going there to be trained to be revolutionaries. Whilst I think some of us might have liked that, for the Cubans it was support and solidarity that they sought and gave, isolated as they were by the total embargo imposed by the United States. British Airways, which in those days was still nationalised, cancelled our flight, but our resourceful organisers,

the Bertrand Russell Peace Foundation, arranged for a Czech plane to fly over to London and replace it. This was the time of the Prague Spring, and some of the countries behind the Iron Curtain were becoming restless and seeking freedom. In Cuba there were over 700 people from many countries, mainly European, but also some Vietnamese, South American, African. The Cubans had built the camp in wooded hills to the west of Havana, a series of raised cabins, with a large communal open sided building in the centre, where food was served. There was also a bookshop, a meeting room and a small medical centre.

The communal dining room on the Cuban camp, 1968:
Photo courtesy of Chris Allen.

We worked in the mornings, from six a.m. to midday. Terraces had been carved out along the contours of the hills. We dug holes with pickaxes, filled them with topsoil and planted coffee bushes and hardwood trees alternately. I loved the work and never missed a day, although it was optional. During the afternoons we sometimes had seminars, and on other occasions we were taken out on visits around the country. The Cubans were extremely generous, the whole trip was free of charge, we had only had to find money for our flights to take us there. We came to realise, to our embarrassment, that we were being given much better food than the average Cuban. We were, though, shocked to discover that Cuban men who had long hair, beards, sandals and jeans were disapproved of, as was rock and roll. All this was seen as Yankee and therefore counter revolutionary. Interestingly only men seemed to be targeted.

We were there for six weeks, and after a while people on the camp began to flex their wings and hitchhike into Havana, as I did one day with a Ghanaian man. He especially wanted to know why there were virtually no black people in the upper echelons of Cuban society, something which I, from my cocooned white ignorance, had not noticed. We visited the poster-making centre. This was a state-of-the-art silk-screen production centre making huge, beautiful, multi-coloured posters to promote health, education, and, of course, political propaganda. Looking back, it seems amazing that the two of us could just roll up there and be welcomed and shown around. The Victoria and Albert museum in London now has a number of these posters in their archives, carefully filed in drawers in acid free tissue paper!

Shortly before we were due to leave Cuba, the Russians invaded Czechoslovakia in their tanks, to suppress the new-found freedoms of the Prague spring. There was just one Czech plane in Havana, and it seemed that once it landed in Prague it would not be allowed to leave again. The Czechs living and working in Cuba were desperate to go home to see if their families were alright. Some of us hoped we'd be stuck in Cuba indefinitely. By now I think the Cubans were anxious to send us home, we were too free spirited. In the end, we were flown back to London, and the plane then returned to pick up the Czech workers. We had been there for two months in all. At Heathrow, we learned that a few people on our flight were to be refused entry and sent back to their countries in Central or Southern

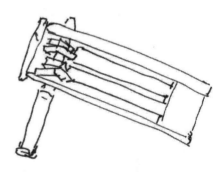

America. Some of them would be imprisoned and perhaps tortured for going to Cuba. We refused to leave them behind, and occupied the transit area for hours, sprawled all over the floors, until the authorities finally relented in exasperation and let everyone through. It was a lesson in resistance and solidarity. I made a number of good friends on that trip, including Sue and Jane.

Most of the women living in the house became involved in the plans for the demonstration, and there were further meetings which included growing numbers of women from elsewhere who were planning protests, some of whom had also bought seats. In addition, there were many groups planning to protest outside the Albert Hall, but our intention was to go inside and create the maximum disruption, and if possible, bring the show to a halt. We discussed strategy, allocated tasks and made lists of all the items we could think of to wreak havoc: flour and stink bombs; smoke bombs from theatrical suppliers; water pistols to be filled with ink, or just water; rotten fruit; football rattles and whistles; and leaflets, loads of leaflets. We trawled joke and toy shops for these items. We experimented, tried things out, and established that the stink bombs indeed smelled terrible, and the smoke bombs could be set off with a lit cigarette. It is hard to believe now, but smoking was allowed in all public places. The smoke bombs, which were sold for use as theatrical effects, were quite safe. We wrote and printed the leaflets in our north London house, which contained a small offset-litho press. The slogan was the brainchild of Sue and was also used on placards carried by people outside the Albert Hall. It said in big, bold black letters 'WE'RE NOT BEAUTIFUL OR UGLY. WE'RE ANGRY'.

At one meeting someone said that the first part of the show was not shown live – it was all filmed the day before, during the dress rehearsal. We hadn't realised this and were very shocked and concerned. We had to be sure not to start before it was live, and we needed to establish very clearly the moment we would begin. We had quite lengthy discussions about the sequence of events, which none of us were very sure about, since we had not been in the habit of watching the show and most of us didn't even have a television. I suggested one person should give the signal, once we knew that the show was live on air. Everyone said, 'Oh yes, that's a good idea, you do that'. I gulped, somewhat alarmed at this responsibility, but having suggested it I didn't feel I could then pass the buck on to someone else. I didn't think of myself as a particularly brazen person. I was shy and introverted, having grown up as an only child and been sent to an all-girls boarding school. It was agreed that I use a football rattle, which was very loud. Somebody had two seats in the stalls, at the end of a row, near the centre and the judges. It was decided that I and the other Sarah would sit there. The night before the contest a bomb was planted under one of the BBC vans parked outside the Albert Hall. At this time small groups in many western democracies were beginning to advocate violent, direct action, impatient with what they saw as the slow, ineffectual progress of protest groups; in the United States it was the Weathermen, in Germany the Baader Meinhof people, in France Action Directe. In the UK it was the Angry Brigade.

We were appalled. After our months of meetings, planning and careful preparations, was everything going to come to naught? The news appeared in the *Evening Standard* newspaper – it had happened too late to be in the daily papers. We read in the *Standard* that security precautions were to be put on a tighter footing. We had frantic discussions; should we call it off, not try and go inside with our bags full of our 'ammunition': the leaflets, the water pistols, smoke, stink, & flour bombs, whistles, football rattle and so on? Would we get past the greatly increased security checks on the doors? It felt like a lost cause. But in the end we decided not to give up, we had invested too much of ourselves in this project. There was nothing to lose. What was the worst that could happen? That we were stopped, searched and arrested for our harmless, if troublemaking, baggage? It was already known that many other protests were planned, by the Young Liberals, and anti-Apartheid groups, as well as by different feminist groups. But they were all going to be outside. We would still try to go in. That bomb greatly heightened the tension for all of us that evening as we approached the Royal Albert Hall.

We had tried to look as smartly dressed as possible. This was a challenge for those of us from our north London house. When we moved there it had been decided that there would be no private property at the house. This covered everything, including clothes. Men's and women's clothes were all mixed up together, including jumpers and jeans of all sizes. There were some lovely things which people brought with them when they arrived. However, there was a steady flow of visitors to the house, in addition to those of us who lived there, and we came to realise that some visitors applied the 'no private ownership' very generously to themselves and went off wearing what were invariably the nicest garments in our stocks, leaving us with the scruffiest selection. I had a coat which I loved

Poster Workshop

and had bought in a junk shop in Brighton when I was at art school there. It was full-length black velvet, fur trimmed with art nouveau embroidery on it, and I wore it that evening. At least it hid my jeans. Soon afterwards it went walkabout and I never saw it again. I carried a large bag slung over my shoulder. It felt conspicuously bulky, but I tried to keep it tucked under my arm. In it were flour, smoke and stink bombs, tomatoes, water pistols, leaflets, a whistle – and the football rattle.

We made our way to the Albert Hall separately, in twos and threes, not wanting to draw attention to ourselves as large groups of women. We gave the protestors outside – there were many of them – a wide berth, lest any of them recognised us and called out.

We tried to look as though we were part of the audience, there for the show like everyone else. Sarah and I got in the queue. When our turn came we pulled out our tickets and presented them in trepidation, and, amazingly, we were through. The vast hall holds an audience of 5,500. Our seats in the stalls were amongst the most expensive. It felt as though we must have stuck out like sore thumbs, surrounded as we were by men in black tie and women in long evening dresses and sleek ermine coats, sparkling in their jewellery.

There was a heady smell of the many perfumes worn by the women, and of the smoke of cigarettes. One of the judges, the Maharajah of Baroda, was smoking a large cigar. The wait was agonising. We were very nervous and the spectacle seemed interminable. The 'beauty queens' were endlessly shunted to and fro. Firstly, each of the fifty-eight women came out one by one, in their country's national dress. Their country and their names were called out, and they walked the full length of the long stage, twirled around and took up a position in a line. It was alphabetical. Miss Africa South was the first.

This was one of a number of controversies that year. Protests against the South African Apartheid regime had been growing increasingly vociferous. There were widespread boycotts of South African goods. South Africa had been forced to leave the Commonwealth in 1961 and had finally been expelled from the Olympics in 1970 for refusing to allow non-white participants in their teams. By then they were excluded from most sporting events. The South Africans decided that they would circumvent a boycott of Miss World by entering two contestants, one white, Miss South Africa, and one black, Miss Africa South. Mecca, the owners of the franchise, accepted this. They were not ones to take a principled stand. Their concerns were more about the contestants being deemed women of virtue: not married, let alone have a child, not sullied in any way.

As we sat watching this interminable parading, my thoughts turned to my very conservative parents, probably watching at home, with no idea of what I was doing. I looked at the people around us, so expensively dressed. My father was a self-made man, and later in his life when he could afford it, he had his best suits made in Savile Row, the king's tailor, he told me (from when there was a king). He was very proud of this and cared deeply about his appearance. His umbrella was always impeccably rolled by the shop where he bought it, and because he couldn't manage to roll it up again to perfection he preferred to walk in the pouring rain, bowler hat and all, rather than open it and then have to take it back to the shop to be rolled up again. Finally my mother managed to master this skill, and he would then sometimes actually allow himself to use it. He was so completely the image of the city gent, even then something of a dying breed, that he was once approached by a French photo journalist on London Bridge wanting to take a picture of him for the cover of a French magazine. My father, ever the discreet Englishman, was horrified, turned him down and fled.

SHEFFIELD VIETNAM DEMONSTRATION

2pm Sat March 1st to Sheffield City Hall assemble Tinsley Wire Sheffield-Tinsley turn-off from M1 **VICTORY & PEACE IN VIETNAM**

Poster Workshop

On the other side of the auditorium I could see Jane and Jo. Jo and I had met just after my return from Cuba, when we each discovered the recently opened Poster Workshop in Camden Town. This was an incredibly exciting place in a dark and dingy basement. Here we made silkscreen posters for radical and revolutionary groups from all over the world, as well as for industrial and rent strikes, civil rights, anti-war and anti-racist movements (notably against the Vietnam war, and against Apartheid in South Africa), student sit-ins and left-wing cultural organisations. It was run entirely by volunteers and there was no fixed charge for posters; people paid what they could afford. We all had jobs elsewhere, teaching, cleaning and so on. Jo and I, and some of the others there, had been to art school. One stalwart of the workshop was a seventy-year-old Cockney pensioner, who had become involved through the long running GLC (Greater London Council) rent strike. He was always to be found there, dressed in a black suit, tie, waistcoat and hat, a cigarette hanging out of his mouth and ankle deep in inflammable rags and discarded paper. Another regular had been in the Merchant Navy for many years. He had left after a long and abortive strike and worked in a Drycleaners over the road. After watching the constant stream of people coming and going, leaving with armfuls of posters or placards, he couldn't contain his curiosity any longer, came over to check us out, and from then on threw himself into helping print posters and keeping us shipshape, as he put it. The Poster Workshop ran for several years, carried on the tide of revolutionary enthusiasm. It was the longest running radical, not-for-profit workshop of that time; Atelier Populaire in Paris lasted fifty days, Berkeley Workshop in California for thirty days. By the time the poster workshop closed Jo and I had become involved in the Women's Liberation Movement.

At some stage we were informed that the show was now going live 'on air'. This was it. In due course the women were tidied away and Bob Hope, the compere of the show, swept out of the wings and took centre stage. He began by reassuring the audience not to worry about the bombing the previous evening, the extra security laid on would prevent any trouble. He then got into his stride with cracks about cows and cattle markets, which the contest had been compared to by feminist critics. He said he liked to go backstage and check out the calves – "moo". Strutting about and warming to his subject, he said that whoever was

THE GREEN BERETS
WITH **JOHN WAYNE** AND CO-STARRING
THE DEAD VIETNAMESE PEOPLE

Poster Workshop

the lucky winning contestant would be taken by him to Vietnam, to be paraded before the G.I.s fighting there – to give them the 'hots', all the better to fight the 'Cong', that is the Viet Cong or the Vietnamese People's Army. Even the audience became uncomfortable and was falling silent.

The war in Vietnam was at its height. Growing numbers of massive and often violent demonstrations against what the US was doing there were taking place across the USA and all over the world. 1969 saw the largest ever American anti-war demonstration in Washington DC, numbering 250,000 people. In 1970 six students were shot dead by National Guardsmen during protests. Tens of thousands of soldiers received dishonourable discharges for desertion, and between 1965-1972 500,000 men had become 'draft dodgers', fleeing the country to evade conscription. By the end of the war 58,200 American men and women had been killed or were missing. Vast areas of Vietnam had been rendered uninhabitable through massive bombing, and the spraying of twenty million gallons of chemicals to destroy the forest cover and food crops used by North Vietnamese and Viet Cong troops. It was estimated that two million Vietnamese had been killed (some say many more), three million wounded, and another twelve million became refugees. (www.history.com/topics/vietnam-war/vietnam-war-history) This was the first war that was filmed and photographed and played out on people's television screens, night after night, as they sat in their sitting rooms. Terrifying pictures of men, women and children fleeing the bombing of their villages, and screaming from the terrible pain of napalm on their bodies.

It was time to go. After a whispered discussion, Sarah and I slid silently out of our seats in the darkness. I made my way down towards the stage and planted myself in the aisle. I turned the football rattle furiously, on and on, for what seemed like forever before there was any response. I felt like the army leader who waves his arm to call his troops to follow him into battle, only to turn round and find there is no longer anyone behind him, he has been deserted and is completely alone facing the enemy.

But in fact our army of women was right there and raring to go. I learned later that nobody was quite ready, and took a while gathering their possessions and lighting their cigarettes to set off the smoke bombs. Then complete pandemonium broke out. Whistles, screams and shouts were coming from all over the auditorium.

The acoustics of the Royal Albert Hall are excellent, the place was ringing with sound. Showers of leaflets were fluttering down from the galleries above. Smoke bombs landed on the stage, smoke rising and spreading up and outwards to mix with the leaflets and the clouds of flour. It was a wonderful spectacle. Bob Hope, after all his bragging about Vietnam, tried to run away. Years later we learned that Julia Morley, co-owner with her husband of the contest franchise, had prevented this by grabbing his ankle. We had been seated very near the judges, and my plan had been to head over there and spray black ink onto the judging papers. Unfortunately, that was not to be. I was grabbed from behind by a burly security guard, lifted up and removed to a nearby room. I was locked in there with Sarah, and shortly afterwards we were joined by Sally Alexander and another woman, who I learned was Margarita. Unbeknownst to us, they had been seated not far from where we were, whereas all the other demonstrators were on the opposite side of the hall. There were policemen everywhere, presumably the extra security forces drafted in to prevent any disruption. (That was very effective.) A policewoman stayed guarding us. I still had the large shoulder bag full of our 'ammunition'. I didn't want to be held accountable for that, and I wandered around the room trying to think what to do with it. Finally I found a chair in a dark corner where I sat down, slid the bag off my shoulder, and pushed it right under the seat. I thought later of the cleaning woman who would find it the next day and wondered what she would make of her discovery. I wonder what the Albert Hall cleaners thought of our protest, which was, after all, about women's rights. They might have just grumbled about the extra cleaning – but still, I like to think it may have given them food for thought. Sally was taken away after a while, and the rest of us were held there till midnight. There were still lots of demonstrators outside, and we called out to them from the windows, waving through the bars. When they realised what had happened to us, that we had been locked up and were being detained, they began chanting and demanding our release. Some of them stayed there until finally we were released. Probably the police couldn't decide what to do with us and had had enough. In the end five women were arrested and charged. Sally was one. Jenny was charged with having an offensive weapon, one of the theatrical smoke bombs.

Jo and Kate, having been thrown out of the Albert Hall, later went to the Cafe de Paris, where a grand dinner was laid on for the contestants, and were arrested for throwing flour and tomatoes at the Mecca henchmen outside. And Mair, who had not been involved at all until she saw it on television, had jumped on a bus and rushed over, only to be grabbed by a policeman as she arrived outside. She told him to 'fuck off' and was charged with offensive language. This was dismissed by the magistrate early on in the trial, which took place in Bow Street court the following February. Jo, Jenny and Kate chose not to have lawyers and defended themselves. All five women pleaded 'Not Guilty'. We had been made to feel guilty all our lives by society, none of them were going to plead guilty now.

The demo had happened too late to make it into the morning papers, and none of us had televisions. Furthermore, in those days there were no video recorders, no 'watch again' or 'playback'.

So although I do remember a great sense of achievement and satisfaction, it was a long time before we fully realised the extent of what we had managed to do, and the impact it had had. We later learned that membership of the Women's Liberation workshop doubled in the month that followed. In other parts of the world, such as Australia, the pageant was screened the following day. Everybody had read in their newspapers about our disruption of the contest and they were expecting to see it. So the BBC didn't dare cut it out!

For Eric Morley and the Miss World Pageant it was deemed a public relations disaster. For us it was a triumph.

'Eve' 1980 © Mair Twissell.

Mair Twissell BORN 1943, IN WALES. DEGREES IN FINE ART PAINTING FROM CARDIFF COLLEGE OF ART AND GOLDSMITHS, UNIVERSITY OF LONDON. EXHIBITION VENUES HAVE INCLUDED THE ROYAL ACADEMY, CARDIFF MUSEUM, GLYN VIVIAN ART GALLERY SWANSEA, AND THE FITZWILLIAM MUSEUM, CAMBRIDGE. SOME OF HER SHORT FILMS HAVE SHOWN IN THE PRIDE AND PORTOBELLO FILM FESTIVAL.

I'm Welsh and I lived as a child in a valley in Wales close to nature, surrounded by mountains, rivers and woods. I was brought up in a caring, socialist family. My father played the piano and my mother sang and often we sang together around the piano. Home life was very lively and full of activity and discussion.

I passed the 11+ to study at the local grammar school and went on to study art in Cardiff College of Art. I felt liberated and that I had found a place where I was not judged by my appearance, I was a person with talent and it felt good. Arriving in London in 1970 with my husband and small child, I was optimistic, ready to take on the art world. It did not take long to discover there were no female artists exhibiting and no matter how dedicated or hard I tried, the odds were against me. The art world was dominated by male artists and I felt angry. At first, I blamed myself for being naïve until I realised there were many other women in the same situation.

The day I was arrested changed my life. I was sitting listening to my radio when I heard there was a demonstration outside the Royal Albert Hall protesting against the Miss World competition and inequalities of women. I knew at once the demonstration was about me. I asked my neighbour downstairs to babysit and I put on my coat and went by bus to the Royal Albert Hall. When I got there, I saw women outside shouting 'down with patriarchy'. I identified with their anger and started shouting too. Two policemen grabbed me and pushed me inside a Black Maria and I was taken to the Bow Street police station, put into a holding cell with four other women: Sally Alexander, Jennie Fortune, Kate McLean and Jo Robinson. I was charged with conspiracy and later obstruction and abusive language and given one phone call. My husband and friend came to the police station to bail me out. It was a frightening experience.

I had a wonderful female barrister called Nina Stanger who was instrumental in getting the case thrown out, but I continued to attend court proceedings to support the others until the end of the trial. Every day the courtroom was packed with women supporting us, chanting and shouting 'down with misogyny' – it was pandemonium. The magistrate, Geraint Rees, kept reprimanding us with no success. We refused to accept the legitimacy of the court because we wanted a woman magistrate. I strongly identified with these women and felt proud to be part of the demonstration. On leaving the court I saw many people cheering us on, including Gay Liberation Front who had put on an alternative Miss World Contest to challenge the stereotype image of women.

I was politicised by the trial and it had a strong influence on my practice as an artist. After the trial, I chose to express feminism through art. The painting 'Egg in Oven' (1973) depicts the suspension of a cracked egg on an oven rack. I see the form of the egg as inherently feminine, it represents womanhood and connotations of life and rebirth. As such, the egg is a symbol of the rebirth of my creativity as a feminist and female artist. On a wider level, while the fragility of the egg's placement on the rack speaks to the precarious placement of women's creativity in a patriarchal society, it doesn't slip down off the rack. I wanted to express a

'Egg in the Oven' 1973 © Mair Twissell

message of strength, that women's creativity and self-expression will survive the pressures of oppression and domesticity.

In the painting 'Eve' (1980), I place the female form in multiple poses, shadowed by the masculine body in an imagined, natural world. Suggestions of trees, sky and moon are patched together around the female figures as an allegory for the representation of women as archetypes. Repeated throughout the painting is the motif of the woman reaching for the fruit trees in a reclaiming of the biblical story of Eve and the forbidden fruit. Through the warm reds and pinks and loose expressive marks I present the Eve figures as bold women filled with life and curiosity, tied to the natural world rather than portraying the condemned, submissive biblical figure.

The women's liberation movement changed many aspects of society. In art, my work was shown in major exhibitions from the Royal Academy of Arts and the Fitzwilliam Museum to Cardiff Museum, The Glyn Vivian gallery, and many more venues, and I was a member of The Welsh Group and SLAG (Surrealist London Action Group).

Jane Grant BORN NEW YORK (1944), CAME TO LONDON AGED TWENTY TO STUDY FILM MAKING AND STAYED. SHE PROTESTED AGAINST THE MISS WORLD CONTEST THEN TRAINED AS A MIDWIFE IN THE 70s AND WORKED UNTIL SHE RETIRED TO LOOK AFTER HER GRANDSON. SHE HAD A MOTORBIKE ACCIDENT AGED 60 AND, AS WITH AGEING, SOME OPPORTUNITIES ENDED, AND OTHERS JUST BEGAN.

On November 20th 1970 the *Evening Standard* reported that a bomb had exploded under a BBC van alongside London's Albert Hall the night before. None of the equipment was damaged, however, so the experience of the 30 million British viewers expected to watch the Miss World contest would not be affected. Meanwhile, 'security precautions were put on a tighter footing'. (*Evening Standard*, 20 November 1970)

In order to avoid drawing attention to ourselves we had agreed to split up before we got to the Albert Hall. I approached the queue that snaked around the building and decided to do whatever it took, in my mind at least, to 'blend in'. I sidled up to strangers and chatted happily in an effort to look like I belonged. Full of a wild-eyed confidence as well as nerves, who knows what I actually said as I approached startled couples.

At the time I was living in a commune in Islington. What to wear posed a problem as our clothes were shared and stored in a wrinkled heap in a cupboard. As much as we wanted to fit in, we had no idea what that looked like, especially for an event like this. In the end I borrowed a smart long navy corduroy coat, kept buttoned up throughout, and boots. I felt confident that I could pass.

Asking someone in the line for a light was a useful tactic in normalising my presence though rummaging through my shapeless cloth bag for a cigarette carried the risk of revealing its contents. By the time the queue began to move I felt weirdly invincible. I signalled 'Bye bye', 'Enjoy the show' to those around me and marched forward.

After entering the building, I had stairs to climb and then to descend until I found my seat. A thigh-high partition formed a continuous barrier between my row and the back row of the stalls with a five-foot drop separating us. The stage was to my left and my seat was about halfway along that side of the hall. A perfect view, but I was beginning to feel exposed and alone. We had thought we would be less conspicuous sitting as single unaccompanied women than in twos or groups and had agreed not to seek each other out in the venue. I avoided turning to look behind me or obviously scanning the room. Furtive glances. I didn't recognise anyone.

The hall was filling slowly and there was time to kill before the event started so I did a mental inventory of my bag:

> *Leaflets*
> *Flour bombs*
> *Football rattle*
> *Whistle*
> *Stink bombs*

I had decided not to take smoke bombs but brought stink bombs instead. I'd heard that anti-war protesters in the US had shut down army recruiting centres with a very potent fluid. I was able to get some and design what turned out to be a very ineffective 'bomb'.

Sue, Sarah and I had met in the summer of '68 on an education and work trip to Cuba with hundreds of other European activists. The Cubans built a camp for us in the Pinar Del Rio. We were trucked into the hills most days to plant trees for precious wood and coffee. I remember an open-air screening of the *Battle of Algiers*. The film was about Algeria's war of independence with France and sitting on a hill alongside North Vietnamese soldiers in Cuba for Rest and Relaxation it was an emotionally charged experience. The Cuban people's pride in their revolution was evident wherever we went.

That May in Paris a revolution had seemed possible and here in Cuba it had already happened in 1959. We came back fired up. Sue, Sarah and I remained friends although our activism took us in different directions – mine was mainly in film.

I had previously edited a film about student power and the 1967 London School of Economics occupation and I'd made a film about the Greater London Council tenants rent strike.

After Cuba, I joined a political film group with others who believed film could be a tool for radical change. This involved making short films, showing them to shop stewards and workers in factories, hoping for their collaboration in production.

Poster Workshop

Poster Workshop

A small group of us organised an Open Festival of Films to run at the same time as the London Film festival. The aim was to bring films to people for free. We used community halls around East London for showings and Sarah (part of the Poster Workshop along with Jo) made us posters that we fly-posted around the area. The Cuban and Canadian embassies let us have documentaries for free. We got hold of a generator to show films outside the National Film Theatre (NFT) and asked directors to withdraw their films from the festival and let us project them instead under Waterloo Bridge. Jean-Luc Godard was the only filmmaker who said 'yes', more out of pique with the festival organisers than in support for our aims. For me the highlight of the festival occurred when the NFT doorman stood between our projector and the screen and said 'this is not allowed' with the image of Che Guevara projected perfectly onto his black uniform. The low point was our generator breaking down and having to plug into the NFT's electricity supply.

In late 60s London there was growing resistance to police repression in black communities, to the policing of Vietnam demonstrations, and anger about the war in general – and with that more arrests. We began organising around the law. Our activism was either in solidarity with other groups or arose from immediate situations in which we found ourselves and we often used direct action in protest. At one point some of us carried out a 'raid' on a mock prison cell in Waterloo Station set up to recruit prison guards, snatching the prisoner mannequin, and taking 'him' to a flat where he gave an interview to the *Guardian* by telephone about prison conditions. We named him 'Ivor Scaped'.

In the summer of '69 I worked with some French activists and went with them to Algeria to the first Pan-African Cultural Festival where they set up the Black Panther Centre, and planned to film an interview with Eldridge Cleaver, recently arrived from Cuba. Several thousand artists and intellectuals from across the continent congregated for ten days celebrating African independence and the future. As film editor I was on the periphery of the group and I was mostly free to attend events, wander around, meet and talk with people. Surrounded by musicians, painters, African leaders and freedom fighters I started asking myself: what was I doing?

I had many reasons to be angry. My mother had killed herself when I was four and from an early age I was angry about the secrets and lies that obliterated her voice and memory. In our fractured family Rita, our nanny, became a mother to us three children. She often took me to visit her Irish mother, aunts and friends who seemed to live in a parallel universe to my own. Growing up in New York City the privilege associated with skin colour and class felt absurd and obscene.

The activism I'd been involved in since arriving in England felt intense and worthwhile but I hadn't yet understood my place in other peoples' revolutions.

Women's Liberation Conference, Ruskin College, Oxford, February 1970: Photo © Sally Fraser

Sarah, Sue, Jo and I heard there was going to be a Women's Liberation Conference at Ruskin College in Oxford in February 1970 and decided to go. I was curious and excited but also apprehensive that a women's

Women's Liberation Conference, Ruskin College, Oxford, February 1970: Photo © Sally Fraser

movement would be 'divisive to the left' – repeatedly claimed in male-dominated meetings. What was extraordinary and new to me was large groups of women talking and listening to each other, for days, over a huge range of subjects. I didn't realise how many men were actually there until I saw photos later. They felt invisible to me at the time. Scarves were thrown over the busts of important men along the walls of the hall.

It felt like home and it felt strange at the same time. Again, I remember being more observer than participant and this made me uncomfortable and probably contributed to me joining others in feeling we should Do something. We painted slogans around the town centre, and one woman painted some in the College building itself. There was a lot of anger the following day from the organisers and other women. I try to remember what the slogans meant to me at the time. 'Women in labour keep capital in power' – was this with reference to employment, reproduction or the Labour Party? Probably all of these.

Back in London Sue, Sarah, myself and other women started to meet in a women's group. Some groups had already started in '69 but the numbers swelled after Ruskin. I wanted to understand better what the conference had meant to me, the effect it had on me, and why? The meetings were like nothing I had ever experienced before. We made sure everyone had a chance to speak with no interruptions and that what we spoke about was confidential. We had all heard of consciousness-raising but I for one wasn't clear about what it was, how to do it or recognise it. As we talked about what most of us had never shared before, suddenly it was there. We began to see in social terms what it meant to be a woman.

I was ashamed of what I had long seen as MY hang-ups and now came to see them as understandable responses to impossible situations and expectations. We could be kinder to ourselves and to each other. Things seemed to move very fast in the group where the emphasis was on 'the personal is political'. We felt we'd been conned as well as complicit and were impatient for change, revolutionary change. There was tremendous solidarity, anger and sadness shared between us for the isolation we'd experienced and the competitiveness we'd felt towards each other. We had confidence in the social significance and revolutionary potential of our anger. As we came to better understand the explanations for our oppression, our solidarity in relation to other oppressed groups became stronger and fiercer too.

In terms of activism we never again wanted to organise in ways that reflected the authoritarian, hierarchical, repressive relations of the society we wanted to change. Robin Morgan's 70s essay 'Goodbye to all that...' (blog.fair-use.org/2007/09/29/goodbye-to-all-that-by-robin-morgan-1970/) was an angry, joyful, and funny critique of the sexist, co-opting, male dominated 'new left' in the States. She spoke for us. It felt like we brought struggle into everything we did. It was a very intense time. And a period when women waking up to patriarchy were routinely accused of having lost their sense of humour.

Women's Liberation Conference, Ruskin College, Oxford, February 1970: Photo © Sally Fraser

Four of us, including Sue and the two Sarahs from

our women's group, decided to live in a commune. We wanted to challenge things in our daily lives that kept women, children, and men oppressed. How could we hope to overturn capitalism if we were unable to confront and to change the internalised oppression and behaviour we reproduced in our everyday lives? We wanted to do both. And we believed this was possible.

We moved into a large house in Islington with four men. How the men came to be there is still debated. At the time I felt so much strength from our women's group that I didn't think it mattered. But it did. None of us had our own room except for one of the men who occupied his favourite. The bedrooms were large and, as more and more people visited the house and moved in, each room had as many as three to four double mattresses on the floor. You slept where you could. The women listened to Dylan, The Band and Neil Young and the men to Leonard Cohen. There were frequent meetings about how things were or were not working. Accusations like 'That's your construction' and words like 'reification' were batted across the increasingly large space between us.

In addition to the house meetings we women continued to meet on our own and to network with other women in and around London. We wanted to do an action together and when the idea to disrupt the Miss World contest in November 1970 came up we embraced it. In 1968 over 200 women had protested outside the Miss America Pageant in Atlantic City. Women threw things they'd been driven to buy and wear in the quest for 'beauty' into a trash can — bras, girdles, curlers. Contrary to legend, nothing in the 'freedom trash can' was burnt because the mayor and police feared the boardwalk would catch fire. In an open letter headed 'No More Miss America' Robin Morgan wrote:

> On September 7th in Atlantic City, the Annual Miss America Pageant will again crown 'your ideal'. But this year, reality will liberate the contest auction-block in the guise of 'genyooine' de-plasticized, breathing women. Women's liberation groups, Black

women, high-school and college women, women's peace groups, women's welfare and social-work groups, women's job-equality, pro-birth control and pro-abortion groups – women of every political persuasion – all are invited to join us...We will protest the image of Miss America, an image that oppresses in every area in which it purports to represent us. (Morgan 1968 in Morris and Withers, 2018)

In November 1969 in London women protested outside the Miss World Contest wearing sashes printed with the following slogans:

Mis-Fit Refuses to Conform

Mis-Conception Demands Free Abortion for All Women

Mis-Fortune Demands Equal Pay for All Women

Mis-Judged Demands an End to Beauty Contests

Mis-Directed Demands Equal Opportunity

Mis-Laid Demands Free Contraception

Mis-Governed Demands Liberation

Mis-Used Demands 24 Hour Childcare Centres

Mis-Placed Demands A Chance to Get Out Of The House

(O'Sullivan 1982)

The Times carried an account of the protest. (28 November 1969)

Outside the Albert Hall a group of straggle-haired feminists stamped about, noses pink with cold protesting about this exploitation of womanhood. They wore flesh pink banners stencilled with Mis-Fortune, Mis-Laid and other slogans. "Equal pay, equal rights, equal jobs now" they chanted. But then when has beauty ever been equal? It was a dark night but could their protests have been jealousy? The demonstrators were from the Women's Liberation Workshop, a name which is something of a contradiction in terms.

Hazel Twort, Jan Williams and other women protesting against the Miss World competition outside the Albert Hall, London 1969: Trinity Mirror / Mirrorpix / Alamy Stock Photo

Although the 1970 Miss World demonstration drew on the strengths of previous protests, there was a major difference with the one we were planning. For the first time many women would be demonstrating inside rather than outside the venue. I remember attending meetings in our house, at the Women's Liberation Workshop in central London, and in a pub in Notting Hill Gate where 12-15 women, pushing tables together for a discussion, provoked barely curbed aggression from several men.

We all agreed that the main aim was to stop or disrupt the proceedings and that we would not do anything or have slogans that could be seen as an attack on the contestants, or that might lead to a violent confrontation. In smaller meetings or as individuals, women planned what to do at the event: shouting and making a lot of noise with whistles and rattles; hurling 'weapons' like smoke, stink and flour bombs, as well as over-ripe tomatoes. We also wrote a leaflet that our housemate Ed printed in the hundreds, to be thrown along with everything else when the signal sounded in the hall.

The leaflet drew a parallel between ourselves as ordinary women and women in beauty contests. In both, women are judged and judging each other, aiming to please, and competing with other women. The leaflet identified Mecca (the founders and organisers of the Miss World Pageant) as small fry compared to big business in using our bodies to sell rubbish and robbing us of our sexuality. We were against criticising or attacking the contestants, but we did address the women in the audience with 'Women watching.......... Why are you here?' The leaflet ended with the slogan that has been associated with the 1970 Miss World protest ever since – 'We're not beautiful or ugly, we're angry'. In rejecting the binary options of seeing ourselves as beautiful or ugly we wanted to challenge all the false choices we faced as women in our everyday lives.

I looked down and across the now full auditorium and recognised Sarah quite a bit lower and to the right of me in the stalls. She was going to swing a football rattle to get us all started. I remembered the discussion a large group of us had about whether it was hierarchical for one woman to signal the start. In another we considered the best material and design for flour bombs - that maximised scatter on impact. Penny sweets bags were the best. Some women recall these discussions with a groaning exasperation, but I found them exhilarating because they were so different from my previous experiences of planning. True the decisions took much longer but everyone had a say, not just those who jumped in quickest and spoke loudest. Everyone seemed to be agreed on the basic principles and aims of our protest but at the same time details were left to individual women and small groups to work out exactly what to do in the Albert Hall. Word of the demonstration spread through the grapevine, as someone has put it 'like a bushfire'. There were no mobile phones or internet and emails then and not everyone had a landline. So we had no idea how many women would be inside.

The audience around me was a sea of overdressed people. The men in dark suits and bow ties and the women in evening dresses and furs, their hair piled high in elaborate styles. The vast majority were male/female couples. It was both familiar and strange to see so many heterosexual couples out for the evening. The concept of dating had become increasingly remote and more recently I had begun to ask myself why I still related to men sexually when I shared so much more intimacy with women?

The rush of adrenaline I felt when the show started turned out to be premature. The first half was taken up with performers singing and dancing and the contestants in national dress. Live transmission wouldn't start until Bob Hope appeared and the contestants were in swimsuits. So I hunkered down for what seemed forever.

My childhood experience of beauty contests was watching Miss America on TV with Rita. My memories are full of mutterings about who we liked best, soda and treats, the warmth of her company and the feeling that we were conspiring against the ever-restrictive new order imposed by my stepmother. The competition felt benign and old-fashioned, even then. A regular family event that most children I knew were allowed to stay up to watch. It is sobering to reflect on how young I was when I started to judge faces, including my own, on a scale of pretty.

Finally, Bob Hope swaggered on to 'Thanks for the Memory' – his theme. Unwelcome memories came flooding back. There was the little skip he did coming on stage or down stairs. He would unbutton his jacket and swing one side open signifying god knows what? He was jaunty, swaggering and smug and I recalled how much I had always hated him. I was warming up and so was he.

He wasted no time in saying how happy he was 'to be here at this cattle market – moooooo' – to much laughter, and that he'd just been backstage 'checking calves' – more laughter. I couldn't get over that people were laughing, were so complicit. Looking at documentary footage years later, I could see that Hope had an arrogant tic of pausing after he delivered a joke, waiting for the laugh that in his mind he deserved. Then his jokes began to fall flat – he'd moved on to the royal family – and perhaps the audience drew the line at that. When this happened he paused even longer and shook his head in disbelief as if he was thinking 'what morons'.

We had wanted to avoid starting our action while any of the contestants were on the stage so this meant picking a moment while Hope was on his own. But how long would that be? When would be the best moment with Hope at his worst? Could he get any worse? Yes. His references to the military and the war in Vietnam have been cut from online resources but we all remember his racist, blood-thirsty comments, as well as his dehumanising characterisations of US servicemen and their lusty gratitude for his tours with that year's Miss World.

I was overcome with rage, shock and anger. I looked at Sarah. She looked stricken. We were sure that Bob Hope's outrageous comments would justify everything we were doing but he had exceeded our expectations spectacularly and it was agony waiting for the signal to start the protest.

Finally, the sounds of rattles, whistles, women's shouts filled the air and leaflets fluttered down from the heights. As much as I'd wanted the protest to begin, I was stupefied when it did and wasn't ready. We were standing now and those who could move towards the stage did so. I threw flour bombs, hitting the black jacket of a man in the stalls below me. Whistle between my lips, I struggled to get the top off a stink bomb vial and in the end had to use my teeth spilling some of the liquid into my mouth. Furthermore, swinging the small vial in front of me dribbled rather than projected the fluid. I saw the man who'd been flour bombed had turned around, lifted his chair, and was shaking it in my direction. My eyes fixed on him. He looked crazed. The woman next to him seemed determined to prove that he had nothing to do with her – and never stirred from looking straight ahead. Meanwhile there was chaos on the stage. The flip chart that Bob Hope relied on for his lines had toppled over in the commotion. He looked baffled initially and then jumpy and scared when a flour bomb landed close to him. We would learn much later that he tried to escape altogether and would have if Julia Morley, Eric's wife, hadn't managed to grab him by the ankle as he fled the stage.

Once it was easy to locate us, the bouncers moved in. I was still whistling and rattling when I was grabbed and dragged up the aisle stairs towards the exit. After turning myself into a dead weight I was just dropped. I was aware of people walking over me, until there was just me, lying on the stairs alone, still in the hall. I went back to my seat and blew the whistle and swung the rattle again. Two bouncers reappeared and I was lifted up the stairs and out the door this time. I had no idea what had happened to other women from my house. We'd never discussed the possibility that we might get arrested or anything about meeting up afterwards. Strange given that we always did this before a demonstration. I decided I might as well go home. Next to all the excitement of planning and the protest itself this felt like an anti-climax. Later that night we heard that the two Sarahs from our house were held until midnight and that in the end there had been five arrests.

Did I care about who won the Miss World title? On the night of the competition we were ejected long before Jennifer Hosten, Miss Grenada, and Pearl Jansen, Miss Africa South, were announced as the winner and the runner-up. We probably heard about this later that night or read it in the morning papers. I remember feeling a buzz that they were both black, but the excitement would have been more at the level of giving the finger to apartheid and to the white establishment in general than about feeling this was important. After all, it was a beauty contest where all of the women regardless of their colour were being objectified, exploited, humiliated, and used to endorse homogenised standards of beauty as well as giving support to industries that promise beauty transformations with their products. Furthermore, women are compared to and set against each other in beauty contests. How can this ever be good? Is the result of a competition based on appearance ever something to celebrate? We understood, at the time, that for some contestants entering and winning a beauty competition offered opportunities they might not otherwise have had, but what were these opportunities? Being groped by sponsors? Accompanying Bob Hope to Vietnam as a 'death mascot' for US troops (Gay 2018)? A relatively small cheque for a year's work? The promise of a career in modelling? And what about the 'losers'? This was probably as far as my thoughts went at the time...my reasons for not thinking or caring very much about who won.

In hindsight it's easy to see other influences on me. Historically the women's liberation movement was predominantly white and middle class. At the time we continued to demonstrate solidarity with black people resisting police intimidation and brutality in the community and knew that black women were organising amongst themselves, but we made little effort to engage over women's issues. Awareness of white skin privilege had a profound effect on me growing up in the States. But the consequence of that was to feel guilt and shame. The women's movement moderated that response through an understanding of my own oppression as a woman. I wonder how different things might have been had there been black women in our women's group? Would we have grasped the idea of intersectionality any sooner? It would take my working as a midwife to understand more about other women's lives and about the commonalities and differences related to race, class, ability, sexuality and the impact of these on health, expectations and choices amongst other things.

In the end four women stood trial with three defending themselves. As a number of us were going to be witnesses we weren't allowed into the courtroom for any of the hearing prior to testifying. We waited with the many supporters in the building and outside in the street.

Jane in the background, with other supporters waiting outside the courtroom, Bow Street Magistrates Court, London, February 1971: Photo © Sally Fraser

Picketing outside Bow Street Magistrates Court, London, February 1971: Photo © Sally Fraser

On the day we might have testified, the judge adjourned the court in response to the constant challenges to his authority and remanded the defendants in custody overnight. The following day they were found guilty, fined and ordered to keep the peace for a year.

Those of us from the house and other women went on to produce three issues of *The Women's Newspaper*. We wanted to draw a line under the spectacular direct action of the Miss World protest and concentrate more on working in the community and building a movement. The first issue came out in time to take on the first women's liberation march in London on International Women's Day in 1971.

Some of us produced a pamphlet *Why Miss World?* to explain our actions both at the competition and in the subsequent trial. It was also an opportunity to critique some aspects such as our failing to engage with the press afterwards leaving an open field for misrepresentation.

In the house our attempts to transform ourselves had become a parody. Sharing the childcare of Kelly and Morgan was the one feature of communal life that was unambiguously joyful, but the dreams I'd had moving in had faded. I fell in love with a woman and moved in with her, her three young daughters, and two other women. I was happy at the prospect of being part of a family of women. In addition to the girls, a boy was born in the summer of '72. The delight of living with children continued for as long as I lived there. Later on I would think that the only way I might have lasting relationships with children was to have them myself. And

I did have a daughter some years later by self-insemination with donor sperm from a friend.

I continued to be active with old and new women friends around squatting and benefits. We ran crèches, summer play schemes and supported the community nursery that Sue and others set up. Some of us did City and Guilds courses in Vehicle engineering and set up a peoples' garage where we invited other women to come, learn about and fix engines. At the time I also wanted a full-time job that offered a more regular income and a sense of being part of something bigger. Having always shied away from joining any organisation, I got a job in the NHS on the ambulance service. I wanted to work in a public sector healthcare role, in a job where women workers were under-represented in the mid-70s and where industrial action was starting to grow. It was my first experience of trade unions from the inside and of monumental sexism in the workplace.

A few years later, along with a number of other feminists, I trained to become a midwife. I was a midwife for thirty-seven years as a

Midwives, women, families, GPs and childbirth organisations march in support of Wendy Savage, East London, 13 June 1985: Photo © David Hoffman.

clinician, lecturer and researcher. The greatest satisfaction always came from supporting women in finding their voices, navigating their paths through the system, and experiencing their own power throughout the whole process and into early motherhood. Since then I've been active around issues related to health or childbirth as an early member of The Association of Radical Midwives organising around education, women's rights, maternity care policy and the profession in the 70s and 80s; campaigning for the reinstatement of the woman-centred obstetrician Wendy Savage whose suspension was engineered by male colleagues; working with a Palestinian NGO to provide childbirth workshops for midwives in the West Bank; and working with Medical Justice to support pregnant asylum seekers in immigration detention centres as well as campaigning to end this practice of detention in England.

I've always been proud of the Miss World protest, although it took me a while to realise what an impact it had made. I've met women who attribute their being feminists to seeing the protest on TV. As a midwife lecturer, I'd discuss feminism with students and if the subject of Miss World 1970 came up there was always someone who would say, 'My mother told me about it' or 'My mum said seeing it changed her life'. When my daughter, Chloe, was at University a lecturer raised the topic of the Miss World protest in a discussion about gender and she blurted out, 'My mum was there'. Her excitement was matched by his. And later, when she related this to me, by my own.

Sue O'Sullivan AMERICAN BORN (1941), HAS
LIVED IN LONDON SINCE 1963. SUE WORKED FOR SPARE RIB
MAGAZINE AND SHEBA FEMINIST PUBLISHERS, TAUGHT IN
HOLLOWAY PRISON AND EDITED ICW NEWS (INTERNATIONAL
COMMUNITY OF WOMEN LIVING WITH HIV/AIDS). SHE HAS
BEEN INVOLVED IN LESBIAN FEMINIST POLITICS FOR YEARS
AND REMAINS A SOCIALIST FEMINIST OF SORTS.

Trying to recall anew the few years before
during and after the
beginnings of the Women's Liberation Movement.
What happenings, contexts, injustices,
histories, emotions, economics, and politics
propelled me into the first trepidatious steps towards
a lifelong mutating affair?

Conjuring up images
discussions, feelings, actions
learning the lessons of my life
other lives
doing and not doing
love and hate
the babies, banalities, marriage, everyday contradictions
I called my life over fifty years ago.

One night trying to sleep on a splintery floor of a church hall
under a piano after a long, inflamed women's liberation conference,

somewhere away from home not missing the kids at all not remembering
anything I would return to
but women's liberation.

No shortage of memories. Some in full colour
Others faded.
Faces emerge, still young
friendships sisterhood
books read gestetner machines grinding out polemics and passion
flats houses and damp buildings
collectives 'She eats collectives for breakfast'
Who the hell was that?
Confusion clarity movement
differences clashes solidarity,
hysteria and tears
sex laughter love
The books and papers we devoured.

* * *

But fuck me. These are not new visions. They are lovingly resurrected,
previously rehearsed – and presented – memories, stories, photos in my mind.
No magic in the recall it's a well-honed skill.
Are they so vivid because I've touched them up so many times over the years?
Do I have a single thing to write about today which I haven't written
about before?
I think I've shot my fucking bolt not once, not twice, perhaps too many
times to count.
In public. In front of people and audiences.

Endless rehearsals
Curated to death
The well-tended archives of an ancient feminist.

Memory is a complicated, slippery, tricky thing.
We hold, weigh and feel the sediment of our lives differently as the sand sifts

Changing times, ageing bodies
brains materiality reality.
My memories faceted tiny pieces of
Flawed beautiful and ugly pictures
the decades weighing in making their own memory marks on my past.

A few years ago while talking about an event in the early years of the
Women's Liberation Movement a few friends and I reminisced, telling
stories about a particular moment in our mutual feminist histories. What had
happened and why and what did it mean?
That sort of older women sisterly talk. Then one friend quizzically remarked
she didn't remember me being there. I was indignant. Of course I was there.
I remembered it so well.
But guess what? That remark niggled.
I dug up some dates, looked at an old diary. There was no denying it – I
wasn't there.
I wasn't there!

Even in 'real time' there are multiple layers to events. Long ago in the 1980s
and within the space of a short time I wrote two separate contributions
for two different anthologies. Both about the same historical moment in
the Women's Liberation Movement. Distinctive stories about one moment
in my life. What elicited and allowed these two strikingly different stories?
Both 'true' but both 'partial'.

Did the uneven ground I stood on while writing each piece elicit different
memories?
or give me different perspectives?
Are my memories all partial? Or at age seventy nine am I losing it? Joking
ha ha.
The self-deprecating self-protecting impulse pushing away the fear.
The returning sadness that what is past for me
is over. I can't live forever. I swear I don't want to live forever.

* * *

I don't remember if I was at any of the Miss World demonstrations. I don't think I was there in 1970.

I had a two-year old and a nine-month old baby in the autumn of 1970.

I know I was at the Ruskin women's liberation conference at the end of February 1970, hugely pregnant. Photos exist. My husband and toddler were there as well.

At the end of 1968 I joined a small group of women which met in Karen Slaney's flat on Chetwynd Road, Tufnell Park.

Initially I wondered whether I could ever climb out of my early motherhood puddle of drudgery and exhaustion and join anything like women's liberation. But after daring to take that first step I was enthralled, engaged, committed. No turning back. No desire to ever turn back. No desire, let alone ability, to shake off any of the exhilarating explosions of

consciousness, politics, connections, passion.

That said, I was still an exhausted drudge in 1970.

So was my husband.

Two kids, two drudges.

I was somewhere present during the Miss World tumult.

There's a photo of me in a line of women protesting the arrests and court case against the Miss World defendants.

Was it outside the court? I look young and demure – not what my memory tells me I looked like at all. Not looking tough and fierce.

Not looking like a drudge at all.

I have a hazy sense, not even a memory, that in at least one
Tufnell Park meeting
we brainstormed more and more descriptive titles for the sashes worn at the Miss World Demo.

Misused, Misunderstood, Misled, on and on they emerged.

But did we do that?

Or did we riff on the 'Mis' words other groups,

other women had already called into being?

Did I long to be at the Miss World demonstration?

I don't really know. It was not the only thing happening in the early
activism of the new Women's Liberation Movement.
Even if I was learning difficult lessons about the delayed gratification
which motherhood brings, I'm not sure.
When our Tufnell Park small women's liberation group decided to
intervene at the Ideal Homes Exhibition at Earls Court in 1969
I was determined to be there. We would engage other women and protest
stereotypes of women's so-called innate adoration of domesticity.
We would challenge our capitalist patriarchal society's manipulation of
women's subordination into consumerism.
But why wasn't I at Miss World – or have I forgotten?
I didn't grow up watching Miss World as a girl. Was I a girl before it even
existed?
I have no memory of giving two hoots about Miss World
especially before the women's liberation movement. Nor did my spirited
friends.
I don't believe it impinged on my girlhood or my teenage longings.

* * *

Fifty years after Miss World I remain a feminist, a socialist in search of
a movement,
a liberationist with a global perspective.
Through many of my decades I remained an ambivalent mother.
I was challenged, am challenged and have struggled
in my daily life, political engagements, dreams, projects, friendships, and
desires with
race
class
sex and sexuality
These among others brought pain and pleasure and sometimes small
bursts of light
Whether collectively or on my own.
Perhaps I could claim I was an activist of some sort.
But for honesty's sake I have to admit that I was always and also
a pleasure-seeking sloth.

I called my 70th Birthday Benefit for Southall Black Sisters the Party of
Resistance.
That was in 2011. Now almost ten years later we're living even more
deeply in – and against – a cruel, austerity damaged society, led by a
bastard upper-class buffoon,
hell bent on destroying whatever vestiges of the welfare state still exist.
Today, as I write in semi hiding at home, we are living and dying in
the global covid-19 pandemic. Join the dots, make connections.

Black Lives Matter uprisings challenge ongoing ingrained racism all over
the world.
Now as much or more than ever we are desperate for new forms of
resistance.
Still longing for women's liberation. Still longing for justice and freedom. I
won't live forever.

The Miss World demonstration in 1970 was a declaration of resistance.
In 1970 Miss World was a technicolour dead-eyed sexist spectacle. A tawdry
cartoon of an event which felt old and encumbered by grey and increasingly
ridiculous men keen to keep control of women everywhere,
revelling in a so-called celebration of beauty and poise.
All for them!

But even then the show was not over, did not die.
Still, today, questions of beauty, whose beauty, defined and used for what
purposes remain.
Young women in ambiguous antagonistic relation to the cartoon
Diversity becoming adorable, decorative.

Our own archived cartoons – full of life and colour and movement.
The white puffs of the flour bombs, the bomb itself, the rattles and the mayhem
signalled a women's rebellion which stepped into that tired yet tenacious spectacle
and attempted to signal Your Time Is Up.

Even if I wasn't there, I will think of it as a collection of others' memories connected to me,
a myriad of jostling interpretations, a part of my political and personal history.
One very public explosion of the women's liberation movement of its time,
created and carried out with courage, drama and commitment.

Sue holding one end of the Tufnell Park Women's
Group banner on Women's march, London 1971:
Photo © Sally Fraser

'Keep young and beautiful',
Women's march, London 1971, L to R
Buzz, Barbara, Michèle, Alison, Sue.
Stills from **A Woman's Place**, 1971,
Liberation Films.

Alison Fell A PROTESTER OUTSIDE THE 1971 MISS WORLD COMPETITION

When we were planning our action the next year – when we were thinking about it – we were aware of the total furore from what happened in 1970. We thought the event might be heavily policed so we'd do a quick tableau – just appear and flash and melt away. So your action affected our planning. I don't think anything went on inside the Albert Hall that year.

Dressed all in black and flashing in the dark. Something that would have a bit of an impact but wouldn't risk our getting bundled off to jail. I think I already had a conviction for insulting behaviour at the Festival of Light earlier that year.

I went to meetings initiated by Jane Arden about forming a women's theatre project. There I met Buzz Goodbody, youngest ever director of the National Theatre. Jane Arden reckoned our ideas were too political and agitprop (Buzz was Communist Party) and didn't accept us into her group. So Buzz rang me up and that's where the Women's Street Theatre Group began.

The first thing we did was on the Women's Liberation march in the spring of 1971.

We had a float and on it we were all shaving our legs and underarms, putting corsets on, face masks on – the whole thing. We were Buzz, Michèle Roberts, Dinah Brook. (I went with Dinah to Oxford Union to talk about Women's Liberation to students and Michèle had come up to me and said she wanted to join and that's how she came to lodge with me and join the group). There was Barbara Hickmott who was an actress and lodged with us as well, and Sue Todd who later founded the Monstrous Regiment Theatre Company. I can't remember who else.

We did a walking tableau to the song 'Keep Young and Beautiful' on the march. We thought the words of the song were so blatant that no one could fail to see that it was ironic.

> *We didn't think of it as a play, we were just dancing down the street. It was just a way of being on the march without just marching. Marching is just tedious and means nothing to the people who see it. But dancing does mean something; it provokes emotion. We think presenting people with images rather than with ideas helps them to grasp ideas better. We liked this particular song and the idea of singing it as we went down Oxford Street. Partly because it's an old song and if you listen to the words of the song they are insane. Any woman who actually obeyed what that song is asking her to do is locking herself up. She's putting herself behind lipstick bars.*
>
> (Audio clip from A Woman's Place, Sue Crockford and Liberation Films, 1971)

And then we did a play in Trafalgar Square. I remember the Maoists shouting and chanting 'Class war not sex war' because I was dressed up as a worker with my tool box from which I produced not a tool but a great big polystyrene penis.

Street Theatre, Trafalgar Square, Women's march 1971: Photo © Sally Fraser

At the Festival of Light later the same year we were dressed up as church, family, and State. All chained together, so very easy to arrest! Especially since we also carried a large banner which read FUCK THE F*M*LY, and both

Flashing Nipple Street Theatre protest outside the Miss World competition, London, 1971: **7 Days**, 17 November 1971, Photo Keith Bailey.

Cliff Richard and Mary Whitehouse were on the platform that day. We were all fingerprinted etc, charged with Behaviour Liable to Cause a Breach of the Peace, tried at Bow Street and fined.

BACK TO THE MISS WORLD 1971 EVENT: We placed ourselves so people saw us as they were coming out of the Albert Hall.

We wanted to point out the objectification of women. We were all dressed in black, sweaters and trousers. I had designed individual wired up systems and cut holes in the jumpers for reflectors around the bulbs. There was a bulb for each breast and a third one for the fanny. I put switches in the pockets of our trousers so at a given signal we would all turn on and flash flash flash. From what I remember there were about six or seven of us. We didn't have any placards or other messages – just the flashing lights. So we could be quite anonymous. Why did we never think of recording all of this at the time? Not sure.

BEFORE: I was in one of the first consciousness-raising groups in Leeds so did some things up there – like invading public bars which were then banned to women. I remember we went to a meeting of the Socialist Workers Party and got into a big argument and used the word sexist and got hooted at and told 'you can't use the word sexist….you're casting scorn on the word racism by using the word sexism'. So I got chucked out of there. That was obviously the first time they'd heard the word said…whereas now we've made the word known by everyone. So I had already been a bit active before coming to London and there was quite a lot of feminist content in the theatre group.

I moved down from Leeds with my husband and Ivan (son) in early 1970. I was trained as a sculptor in art college and was in a theatre group called The Welfare State. I did a lot of costume and stage design as well as writing scripts and songs and dancing.

I came down to London before Roger (my partner) did, before he got a job at St Martins, because I really explicitly wanted to do women's theatre. I don't know why? It must have been something in the air. I remember living in Clerkenwell with my parents-in-law in early 1970 and going off to this meeting that Jane Arden organised and it all started from then. I think I was a bit of an anarchist-Stalinist then with a touch of feminism.

I wish I could remember when I met Sally (Alexander), maybe it was when I joined Red Rag. I'm just in touch with Ros Delmar at the moment. She's been sending me stuff — cartoons that I drew at the time. She's trying to get me to remember all sorts of things and I can't remember anything.

Natasha Morgan BORN IN LONDON 1945. STUDIED ENGLISH AT OXFORD. CREATED THAT'S NOT IT THEATRE COMPANY IN 1978 AND WORKED ON SPARE RIB. IN 1990 SHE TRAINED TO BE A PERSON-CENTRED COUNSELLOR, THEN AS A GESTALT PSYCHOTHERAPIST. SHE WORKS IN PRIVATE PRACTICE IN LONDON.

I was brought up in a family of communists and went on marches with my dad and collected signatures with my mum. Being communists on the one hand and Jewish on the other, I grew up taught not to trust policemen. Or politicians. My father worked for the Daily Worker doing design and layout. I remember seeing the paper come off the press. Dad would load up a bundle and then we would go off on his bike with the day's editions on the back and sell the paper at Wembley Station.

Natasha on demonstration against anti-trade union legislation, London, 8 December 1970: Photo © Sally Fraser

I went on Aldermaston marches and became interested in folk music. My university years at Oxford were mainly spent in theatre and folk singing.

Getting involved in women's liberation seemed so obvious to me and natural in the late '60s. It brought things in my past together, made sense of them and gave me a sense of direction. Growing up I never liked beauty pageants – women as commodities. I went to Miss World with Midge McKenzie (filmmaker) and Kate Millet (author) in 1970. We were in the fourth row of the stalls. I didn't recognise anyone else I knew. I think Midge may have got hold of those seats because of her film-making.

At the time I used to go and buy fabric and make clothes for myself, so I made a replica of a Mary Quant dress that I'd seen. It had a short skirt with a zip-up top, made of a stretchy lime green material and I wore it with pale lilac tights. My father said all I needed was a thing on the top saying tuppence off. I loved it.

I didn't feel the Miss World protest was anti the women contestants. I didn't feel sorry for them. I felt angry but not specifically with the women. They seemed like decorative accessories to financial capital. I think it was the commercialism of it, the commercialisation of the women that disgusted me.

I don't remember a signal. I don't know if we even knew there was going to be a signal. I remember there being some hoo-ha about the possibility of a bomb, so we threw the eggs and tomatoes at Bob Hope quite early on and then rushed off and I went straight back to Dalston. Somehow LBC got our number and wanted to talk to me about what had happened. It felt exciting, it felt empowering talking on live radio. I've always felt good about having been there and having had a part in the run up to it and in the doing of it.

My mother called almost immediately after LBC radio to tell me my grandmother had just died. It was a sudden shift. I left London the following day to help with funeral arrangements.

Since then, and in no particular order, I worked in the *Spare Rib* collective editing letters and reviewing plays. I worked with a women's theatre group and wrote plays about abortion and other women's health issues. We put these on in hospitals. I also worked with an experimental theatre company called The People Show. The most satisfying theatre experiences came with forming my own company. I received Arts Council funding and wrote and acted in my own plays with non-professional performers. Several of these were put on at the Royal Court and the Oval as well as going on tour. The last play I did with my company was prompted by my three-year-old daughter's question, 'What happens when we die?'

I tried to get some work to research anything that would allow me to think about death.

One of the places I went to was a bereavement service run by The Family Welfare Association, and that's where my interest in psychotherapy came from. Rather than make up stories, I realised that the people I worked with had their own stories and needed to talk about them. So I started training to be a psychotherapist. I was a single parent and managed to get funding to cover my training. After I graduated I became a trainer/teacher. I stopped teaching a couple of years ago but still practise as a therapist three days a week.

I miss my feminist friends, hugely. And I miss my writing and theatre work. Lately I have begun to wonder what I might do next.

Jo Robinson MY WINNING FORMULA – TO QUESTION
AUTHORITY USING ART, THEATRE, HUMOUR, POSTERS,
GRAFFITI AND FEMINISM – WAS PORTRAYED MISCHIEVOUSLY
BY JESSICA BUCKLEY IN THE FILM MISBEHAVIOUR. NOW
LEARNING TO MAKE MY REBEL CONSTRUCTIVE, TAMING MY
INNER DRAMA QUEEN AND SELF-DIAGNOSED BIPOLAR STATE,
INSPIRED BY GROWING GLOBAL NETWORKS OF FEMINISM TO
CONTINUE THE STRUGGLE THAT WE MUST NEVER GIVE UP!

Born in Blackpool, Lancashire in 1942, in the middle of the war,
a war baby in a safe place where the troops trained on the
beaches. Brought up on rationing but supplemented with extra
food from the Black Market in Blackpool a seaside resort – where
there were no black people.

My parents were both from working-class families. My father,
Harry Robinson, worked on a Market Meat stall. In 1930 they
married secretly in a Registry Office but they continued to live at
home with their parents. Eventually they had a white wedding in
1936. I was the only child.

Blackpool was seasonal and the trippers from the 'dark satanic
mills' came in Wakes weeks for 'Jugs of Tea on the Sands' in this
working class Tory town, dominated by the phallic Edwardian tower,
surrounded by seven miles of 'golden' sands and sewaged sea. No
trees, no caves, in a flat exposed landscape, Blackpool is a what- you
-see is- what- you- get sort of place, Like-it-or-Lump it, is what they
said. Bracing the breeze, so strong it could lift your spirits right over

the Tower and the dull grey sea. The Arctic wind could flail you to the floor with lashings of wet sand on goose-pimpled skin. You could hear the lions roar in the Tower Zoo and Elvis music drifting out from the Arcades.

My parents, bless them, did their best. They scraped together to better me and I was packed off with a trunk to a nearby boarding school in the very posh St. Anne's-on-Sea to rid me of my Lancashire twang, get a good education and prepare me for the marriage market. Feeling a mixed bag as I moved from working-class Blackpool to middle-class St Anne's-on-Sea. Boarding school was a tough challenge to my spoilt 'only child' existence with no relatives around. I survived by learning to socialize with other children and it really gave me something I didn't realize I had been missing – not having any siblings, I had never had my edges knocked off.

The first 'help' I got was a new 'parent', a 'housemother' who was a bully, not a mentor. I had to get my own act together and quickly developed survival skills to rebel against the rules holding me down, which proved in the end to be my Winning Formula. Laughter was our secret weapon; we had endless supplies of laughter to fuel it. Escape came when I passed my 11-Plus, a crude and biased test of 'Intelligence' to sort out the riff from the raff, which I cracked using my visual powers. I got to the grammar school factory, left boarding school and became a day girl but this meant sharing the bedroom with my mother for my teenage years.

BECOMING A WOMAN UNDER THE PATRIARCHY

What a Bloody Miracle it seemed when I FINALLY reached the menarche, signifying my fertility Rites of Passage for the world to know – potentially a Golden Moment for a Big Celebration – or at least the building of a menstrual hut, but yet sadly, a practice not heard of in my 'tribe.'

'DON'T LET YOUR FATHER SEE!' whispered my mother, pushing me into the bathroom. Then she gave me the 'Got-to-Grin-and-Bear-It-Talk' announcing 'You'll be On the Rag for the next thirty years – but you're lucky to have pads now! Tampax are only for married women and what do you know about sex?' Mother asks me bluntly. 'Why? What do you want to know?' I cheekily retort as I never saw her as a fountain of knowledge, since she had once informed me that sex was like a red-hot knife going through you.

Could the menarche have been the Golden Moment for the real sharing of what it means to become a woman, by bonding and growing over the rites of passage? Difficult as I felt I hardly knew her after the long gap at boarding school and now having to share a bedroom with her. It was a house of strong smells. Everything was put in bowls or jugs under the bed. Bloody rags were left standing in cold water to loosen and the blood would dissolve and sink to the bottom into dark red sediments that smelt like our wet rusty iron gate. When my father was ill, he had a jug by his bed to collect his phlegm, lime green strands, which would be left for my mother to empty in the morning as part of her duties, so he didn't have to see them. We could hear my father's racking cough keeping him awake night after night. His pomaded hair stank out the bathroom.

It was a strange home; you never knew what might lie under a lid or a dish. There could be mildew inside a milk jug, wet tripe under a dish, old porridge in the pan, a carcass of meat (for the black market) in a wardrobe. Of course, I did not know about the idea of Patriarchy but I could feel that home was run by my father's rules, which my mother and I obeyed without question. There were so many things you couldn't let him see. It was easier not to question.

'Patriarchy fills the home'

Mother named me Norma after the

film-star Norma Talmadge, an actor *and* a producer (very rare then) who, accidentally stepping in wet concrete in Hollywood, started the tradition of star's footprints. I like being named after a mistake and one of the few role models for women at that time, but for mother, she was a star. My mother loved sunbathing and taught me to sing: 'You are my sunshine my only sunshine', and she loved dressing me up as Shirley Temple! But I wanted to be a Tomboy because you could play in the mud or climb up trees. My father treated me more like a boy and taught me golf and how to drive, so of course, he was more fun.

I had woven a story about my mother as the Baddy until I found out how he had started an affair just after she had given birth, with the young woman with the iced blue sparkling eyes from next door. Everybody knew! He had been blackballed from the Golf Club. I thought my Dad could do no harm. He was my Beloved Dad who was funny and made people laugh. Yet I had seen that he would never give her any money for herself. He would turn around to count out the housekeeping money from his back pocket. She said there was never any left over, which meant she had none, because she wasn't added into his equation. Her work didn't count!

They existed in an unfinished row that dwindled into ever-lasting silences lasting for days. Notes were left 'Where's the housekeeping, the coalman's coming today?' 'Your tripe and tomatoes is in the cold box.' (But maybe my mother had hoped that this dish was like 'revenge', a dish best eaten cold! And perhaps it gave her respite from cooking on Mondays?). They were like two bookends looking away from each other, with me squashed in between.

I never felt a look of regard from them together. It was always separate, in a one-way triangle with me in the centre between them. No wonder I ended up cross-eyed. So I began to wonder if my only way of escape would have to be via my mother's dream for me? Engaged at eighteen, marry at twenty-one, babies at twenty-three?

She had dreamed her life away with ads like the 1950s jingle from the LUX Liquid Soap. Promising to be 'mild on the hands' that did all the housework. But the dreams had faded. She developed bulbous arthritic fingers and began a decline, the fate for many women in their menopausal years who took a lot of pills for this and that. She was prescribed Phenobarbitones, the first of the tranquillisers that dead-ended you. My uncle inherited their family money, leaving nothing to my mother. When my father died he left everything in his will to me. Disinherited twice, and not able to divorce, she had become a victim in a society that devalued women.

Writing now I see her victimisation came from a powerful patriarchal family structure where no affection was ever shown – no hugging in the overpowering war mood of austerity and rationing. Difficult for a woman then to be a natural in the matriarchal role. I have had to learn how to love my real mum by letting go of the distrust

'1950s Knitting Pattern for the Patriarchy'

and hatred I had wrongly misjudged her with. Much later I started to unravel the patriarchy I had grown up in.

Mother's grooming attempts. I remember being dressed up by her for a party at six years old. Sticking me into this cold taffeta dress with a frilly net top, hating the cold blue material against my skin, whilst she adds the finishing touches, a headband of tiny rosebuds.

'Party Time in 1948'

Then I'm put in front of the photographer and asked to look up for the camera. As I do so my eyes cross because my lazy left eye cannot move any faster and catch the other one up and my mother tuts and the photographer has to rearrange the shot. My mother does more fussing and rearranges the headband. Suddenly a sharp rosebud stalk pricks my forehead and a trickle of blood rolls down one cheek. When it's finally all over we go home and I rush out to play in the party dress, which soon gets splattered with wet soil in the garden. My mother looks out and screams. That's where it all started with the fairy tales for me. Right there.

When I'm a teenager, my mother puts penny coins in between my ankles, calves and knees to see if they can be held there like a Bathing Beauty would have to for the local Blackpool Beauty Contest and thus make a beauty queen out of me! But she looked disappointed when the coins fall out onto the floor.

I wanted her to leave me alone and as a teenager I learnt to sew so I could create my own fashions and began to experiment. I still really wanted to be an artist but you couldn't get a grant to study art outside your town so I stayed for the three year Fine Art and Design Course in Blackpool.

Our tutors took us on a trip to London, singing along with the radio 'Hit the road Jack!' as we sped along the new Motorway to the bright lights of London and to see the exhibition of *The Young*

Contemporaries. My sights were now set on 'Swinging London'.

RUNNING TO LONDON

Both my parents died, my father first. Then I had to arrange my mother's funeral by myself. I locked up the house, left all my possessions, and fled to London. I had my first Chinese meal and watched the Demo in Grosvenor Square against the Vietnam war and the students uprising in Paris '68 on TV. I didn't feel at all connected. I felt like the Oik from Blackpool. I didn't fit in. I made a suicide bid. Hospitalized. Recovered. Became a Scenic Artist and Set Designer.

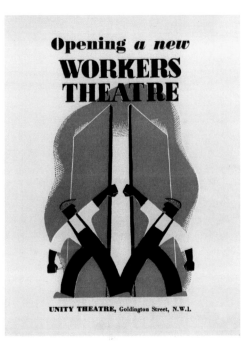

'Where it all began in 1968'.
Poster © Unity Theatre Trust

Whilst I was designing and painting a set at Unity Theatre in Camden Town I chanced on a meeting that was to change my life forever. It was the founding meeting for Agitprop organized by Sheila Rowbotham and John Hoyland, who were planning an event for a festival in Trafalgar Square in support of Vietnamese people. I had a baptism of fire that day, meeting all these people who had become politicised after going to Cuba and from being on the barricades in Paris. They could talk the talk and nearly all had been to university. I learnt that they had been part of change through political action and saw it was now possible to change the world here! So it hadn't been my fault! It was the system's fault and that could be changed.

Agitprop wanted input from artists. Wondering how on earth I could be part of this, since I knew only scenic artist skills, I gingerly volunteered that I could paint tall walls of a building very quickly with red paint and slogans, which brought cheers. Suddenly I saw how art could be harnessed against the state, just as Agitprop was saying. Here I met and was inspired by the brilliant activist and anarchist Cartoon Archetypal Slogan Theatre (CAST) nicknamed 'Jesters to the Revolution' who 'embraced arts labs and community halls, working men's clubs and trades union meetings. Theatre would invade public spaces, redefining the streets as sites for Marxist agitation and Carnivalesque celebration. Gender, race and sexuality were the fault-lines around which radical politics would be redrawn. CAST's particular contribution to the development of revolutionary struggle would be to explore through theatre the problematic relationship between the revolutionary intelligentsia and the working class, between theory and practice'. *'Jesters to the revolution—a history of Cartoon Archetypical Slogan Theatre (CAST), 1965-85', Theatre Notebook, B. McDonnell, 2010*

THE POSTER WORKSHOP
61 CAMDEN ROAD
• BELONGS TO THE PEOPLE
• NEEDS THE PEOPLE
• FIGHTS FOR THE PEOPLE
YOU'RE THE PEOPLE. USE IT

Poster Workshop

Soon after I met Sarah and we joined the Poster Workshop in Camden.

In their dingy basement Workshop I met a student who had come straight off the streets of revolution

Jo and Sarah in Victoria Park, London, before a demonstration against the anti-trade union White Paper 'In Place of Strife'.

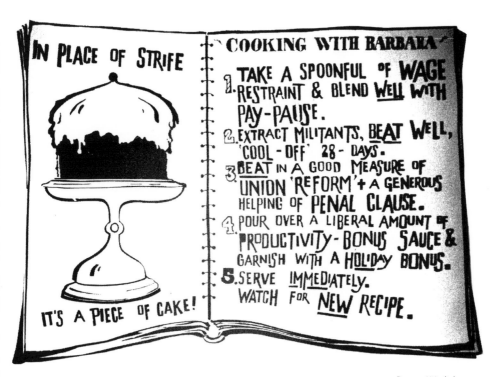

and direct action from Paris May 68 where posters had declared 'If you're not part of the solution you must be part of the problem!' I set to work on my first posters and thought there could be a revolution here any minute now in this electric, do-it-yourself atmosphere which questioned everything, and when you didn't get an answer, Direct Action was taken. Occupations sprang up, Wild cat strikes, sit-ins, teach-ins, student revolts, rent-strikes, eviction resistance, and squatters' campaigns. We plunged in and designed and printed posters for campaigns against injustice, inequality and for liberation.

My eyes began to open to the growth of women's liberation, as sisterhood grew all around me and I went to the first ever Women's Liberation Conference in the UK , launched by women historians in spite of the derision of their male colleagues (but supported by the men holding a crèche for children).

The conference started with how women had been hidden from history, yet they had often started revolutions and that female liberation was the basis for social revolution. Can you imagine how exciting it was to meet and share these ideas with other women? I began to feel even more fired up hearing from other women about the particular ways women had been oppressed.

'Juliet Mitchell and Jan Williams sharing a great idea at Ruskin?' Photo ©Sally Fraser.

The most startling paper was presented by two women with children from South London on 'Women and the family' about women's role in the home, which really prized open my mind visually to the power battle that begins in every sink of dirty pots.

but...
inspiration
Came when...

THE
POLITICS
OF
HOUSE-WORK

appeared in the
FAIRY LIQUID
SUDS

'Inspiration appeared in the bubbles'

A women's consciousness-raising group started up afterwards but I was wary of people who were wanting to 'couple-bash'. I went along but didn't reveal much in the very personal heart-to-hearts sharing. I felt more interested in the liberation of human beings and sexuality being a part of that. I was set on an idealistic search, so never questioned my own real sexual and relationship needs and was still acting as an apologist for male sexist behaviour.

THE PERSONAL IS POLITICAL

But when 'The Personal is Political' slogan first appeared, this was a defining moment in women's liberation for me – like a lightning rod it shot through the meaning of the personal and the political worlds of women. We began questioning rigid stereotypes and how they imprison us, but this also led us into much deeper questioning about how the global oppression of women has been constructed.

This meant we would no longer confine ourselves to politics with a small 'p' (meaning only personal problems) and opened up our relationship to POLITICS WITH A BIG 'P', able to strive for real equality, for real power which could only happen if we began to empower ourselves. But how did we do that? We became informed and empowered by the outflow of women's writings such as *Our Bodies Ourselves* written by The Boston Women's Health Collective in USA in 1970, which was both a radical and do-it-yourself game-changing book which dared to write and show practical information about women's health and sexuality.

'Where do we start?'

Consciousness-raising groups were the backbone of women's liberation. 'Telling it like it is' meant opening up to each other. I become politically conscious as a woman and knew that personal problems could never be solved by individual action, using tears, sex or manipulation.

Empowered by women's liberation, we began to share our anger together. I realized that for me this anger had been boiling up from the moment I became a teenager and resisted my mother's plans. In London I had been drawn to the polished but unachievable icons of beauty in Vogue. But with my new feminist gaze I rejected this as I could see that it prevented me from developing and valuing my own confidence. So I was thrilled to hear the idea of the Miss World contest being targeted and especially with the slogan that questioned the idea of women being designated as either Beautiful or Ugly. I questioned too, the notion there could even be ONE Miss World. Together we had seen that this competition divides us as women. We wanted more than fame for one woman. We wanted liberation for all women!

'New feminist gaze'

MISBEHAVING AT THE ALBERT HALL

I had just started my first serious relationship, moved up to Manchester and soon was pregnant, but I went down to London for the Miss World protest and then I had to return to London for the trial so I left a house again suddenly, and never went back, even for my possessions. I took shelter in the commune in Grosvenor Avenue, Islington. And my never-ending thanks went out to the women who took me in and supported me.

I was twenty-eight and feeling euphoric about being pregnant for the first time. Having become an orphan recently, and the rest of my family all dead, followed by my new relationship with Chris, the father, who was also an orphan, meant we both felt joyous about a new life coming to us.

Getting ready for Miss World. I need to look smart in order to buy a ticket. I dress as though I am going to Ascot (to fit in with the posh Kensington crowd) and put on a pink corduroy coat and a large pink floppy hat. I grab my big leather satchel, containing my arsenal, hoping I do not get arrested tonight.

The Miss World contest was not harmless fun. It was a celebration of sexism. Women are sexually objectified – putting their goods on the table and flaunting their wares and it's as old as the hills. There were always beauty contests of one sort or the other: nymphs lined up for the Minotaur to devour, May Day virgins dancing round the Maypole (early Pole-dance?) before the rape finale. It's such an old game, and so why did we want to be party poopers? With my new feminist eyes it seemed more like a cattle market. Numbered and ticketed, limbs being eyed up for softness or firmness, girths measured, deportment judged. A beauty contest exists in its own bubble of safety by being labelled as 'Family Entertainment' which builds audiences (as long as no one breaks the spell and denounces the Emperor's new clothes!). For the contest to work, it needs a compliant family audience.

I queued up and bought a ticket without any problems, looking up at the vast expanses of the Albert Hall – far bigger than I remembered – I couldn't see anyone I knew. I found a seat in the stalls. It then began to dawn on me that unless I could spot someone I knew ... it was going to be me...doing this ON MY OWN!

Women's liberation had changed my life, so what could it mean for women here, when in a few moments this whole scene will be changed when we stop this show. There will be no going back as the genie bursts out of the bottle and this unequal and sexist world will have to change. Right now I'm scared out of my wits, my heart pounding as I will have to reveal myself to all these strangers as a protestor in their midst.

The show is beginning and the judges enter. I quickly check my satchel for my comic 'arsenal': some soggy lettuces and squashed tomatoes wrapped in cellophane (traditional Music Hall Fayre), a bag of plain flour, some leaflets, a water pistol containing ink and a Joke shop smoke bomb and stink bomb.

Bob Hope enters. His humour depends on old sexist jokes fed to him by teams of joke-writers, who had only worked on Radio with him. This limits him to reading from a script, which is underneath him in the prompt corner. He starts reading off his old jokes but his audience responses are slowing. Oh I can't take his crude and arrogant performance. I can't believe what I am hearing and how much longer will I have to listen to his sexist ranting when at last the signal starts. **YES! THIS WAS IT!** Starter's orders! The rattles start growling. The moment **HAS** come!

'Vision of the genie (in her marigold gloves) freeing herself as she raises the roof off the Albert Hall'.

I join in and scream into the exciting frenzy now taking place all around me and laugh as I see the spectacle getting smashed as more and more flour lands on the stage with a lovely plopping sound. Bob Hope has run for cover as more flour bombs land and then one with a direct hit – knocking over his prompt stand! Mecca Security staff are rushing around the stage but unsure what to do with this guerrilla-style attack that has broken out across the Hall.

I head down towards the stage to see where I can aim my stuff. I see the Women's Liberation Banner has been unfurled in the back of the stalls with women cheering around it.

I open my satchel and select some lettuces and tomatoes. I spy the sexist newspaper reporters in the media scrum and think they could do with some more information about us, given the sexist and racist abuse, inaccuracies, and demeaning writing they concoct about women in general. I pick out a leaflet, add some rotten tomatoes and limp lettuces and begin to lob them, shouting, 'Take that! Read this!' then quickly head into the safety of the stalls.

Time seemed to have slowed and I become aware that the hall has gone very quiet. The shouting has died down, I am now the only protestor, left on my own and stuck right in the middle of the Albert Hall. Somehow I have to get out. The only way out is where I entered. It seems a

'My arsenal imagined as an X-Ray'.

long ascent through the audience, up the steps of the aisles towards a far-off green Exit light at the top of the auditorium.

I begin to cross an aisle full of people but there is a large bouncer in evening dress heading towards me. I search the satchel and grab the water pistol. I hold it up and then turn towards the advancing man and point it at him. The audience in the next row gasps. He is racing towards me and is now in front of me. I pull the trigger and out shoots a stream of blue ink (I had forgotten I'd put blue ink in – thank goodness it wasn't red) It hits his starched white shirt and lands making a blue arc.

I toy with the idea of trying to complete the circle and make my scribble into a women's sign but change my mind as he advances towards me. He pauses to look down at the blue ink and stops dead in his tracks, seeming to freeze. So did everybody else and I thought it's now or never, so I shot up the remainder of the steps and out into the street outside the Albert Hall. As I passed the Gay Liberation Front's carnival but ironic beauty parade, I saw a cow's head trying to team up with its body.

At first I ran, then decided to slow down, hoping no one was following. I got quite a way and then heard footsteps ringing out, coming nearer. A man began to chase me. I ran out into the road and he ran after me and tripped me to the ground.

He was a plain-clothes policeman. He seized a prescription form with my name on it from my bag. He said he thought I must be a drug addict. He began questioning me, when my friend Jane ran over shouting, 'Leave that woman alone, she's pregnant!' I told him this was true, and it was a prescription for my iron tablets. He released me, immediately adding, 'Now go home and don't be silly, be sensible and get the bus home.' But as ever, being labelled 'silly' and cautioned to 'be sensible' and advised to 'go home' only acted as an incentive: **THERE WAS MORE WORK TO BE DONE!**

GLF protesting outside the Albert Hall, November 20th 1970, 'Cattle market parade. A head looks for its body'

I met people at the Bus Stop who said they were going to Piccadilly to continue with the protest. Outside the Café de Paris I joined in a small crowd that had gathered to shout 'Mecca pimps!'. I borrowed a cigarette to light the paper fuse of the yet unused and final weapon, the joke shop smoke bomb, and aimed it away from the crowd onto the pavement. Then I felt the strong arm of the law upon me. We were taken to Bow Street Police Station and charged with Breach of the Peace and Discharging a Missile with intent to endanger the public. We were banged up for the night with the working girls in the next cell, who advised us to plead guilty and 'get it over with quick, love'. But we weren't in the same game and explained that in fact 'we were just getting into it'.

Our Direct Action had lasted only about ten minutes, but we had achieved our aim, even beyond our wildest dreams. **SUCCESS!** We had stopped the spectacle, upstaged a sexist patriarch, and driven him off the stage in a cloud of flour. It was ten minutes that rocked the world for women by launching Women's Liberation on television across the globe and turning many women into Feminists!

AFTER THE CONTEST – THE TRIAL LOOMED

After the summons, I looked carefully at the charges. One was for Breach of the Peace. The wording of the charge used the generic 'he' all the way through. I thought that was a good place to start, by saying that 'he' definitely did not mean 'she' and why was a generic term used anyway to describe and supposedly include women? The whole process of law had employed these terms for hundreds of years, and everybody had complied ever since. Why should we? I also remembered the words of the women who were in the cells, 'Just plead guilty love and get it over with quick.' So that was the preferred norm to follow, and it was what society expected. But we had other ideas and prolonged the trial in a Magistrates Court in order to gain publicity about Women's Liberation.

We met the barristers who had offered their help. One of them showed interest in the issue of gendered wording and went away to consider it but later she withdrew. At that point, I thought we could not expect barristers to pursue our case along the lines we wanted to take so self-defence seemed to offer us much more scope.

MISBEHAVING IN THE TRIAL

As it got nearer to the trial, we had different degrees of anticipation. I was always up for ultimate exposure. I think I probably had to be reined in. I was cross-examined over the offence of 'Discharging a Missile', the smoke bomb bought in a toy shop. When I was asked to read out the instructions by the Prosecutor: 'Light fuse and stand clear!', I could see how that might condemn me. So I did as he instructed me, but read the first part as 'Light fuse and stand!' I then paused and added: **'Clear?'** I could see how using self-defence could be fun.

We questioned the authority of the court at every opportunity. We decided to call the magistrate 'Daddy O'. We refused to conform to his expectations. We shouted out quite a lot, we would not sit still. We talked together and we laughed out loud. We were quite outlandish and tried to hold up the proceedings whenever we could.

The magistrate started out as a comic uncle. But he got crosser and crosser with us and finally stated there were to be no more interruptions Or, he said, banging down his gavel, we would be sent down for the night! I did not heed this, much to everyone else's anxiety, I found yet another objection. The minute I made it, he interrupted with his gavel – DOWN FOR THE NIGHT. The police surrounded us. They tried to grab me, but once again I used the toilet excuse (a pregnant woman's right to choose!) and on his refusal I squatted down. The police moved forward but Sue came to my defence. We were carted off for the night in a Police Van for 'B and B' in Holloway Prison to be taught a lesson, but it was another kind of lesson that night, to witness the conditions for women in prison.

I took the whole thing of going to Holloway as a joke. Boarding school at an early age meant I was used to dehumanising treatment to scare you into submission. We were separated and put into the 'horse-boxes', de-clothed, de-loused, de-personalised. A big game to humiliate. I couldn't wait to see the others and laugh about it because that is how we had fought punishments at school. 'Don't let them grind you down'- keep laughing!

A screw said to me that we were considered 'political prisoners' which seemed a bit of an up-grade to me. I remember them bringing us a cup of tea and a sticky bun, like a treat? After that we were led to the wing and offered a choice of cells! There was no chance of sleep. Many women were calling out across the cells and the wings all night. There were arguments, sobbing, singing and gossip. You could hear bits of their lives and realized that they were in for much longer, than we would be and with a very different outcome. We were privileged middle-class women who had been a bit naughty in their eyes who would soon be out and back in society. But the lesson we had learnt that night stayed with me.

The next day, back in court the Magistrate wrapped it up quickly. We were adjourned for sentencing and all found guilty. The Women's Liberation Workshop generously paid our fines. I have no regrets about our action or about the trial, especially as some of us conducted our own defence. OK, we were found guilty in the eyes of the law, for our ten minutes of action but the impact of that night has lasted over many years. And I met some wonderful women at that iconic moment of women's history whom I have remained friends with ever since because we built a unique and enduring bond together based on rebellion.

AFTER MISS WORLD

Back to our grass roots of action and campaigning, where we all continued the fight against sexism in everyday life and I remember how (in the words of Carol Ackroyd, veteran of Keep our NHS Public) 'We were never interested in breaking through the glass ceilings to join the men in power, we wanted to destroy patriarchy and create a completely different egalitarian world.' I became a midwife and one of the founders of Radical Midwives, campaigning to protect the role of the midwife and to keep our maternity services safe.

After our protest I was keen to keep our story 'alive' with interviews whenever we could. This goes back to school days when I had a wake-up call about how history is created. I had only been taught a biased and boring history of kings and emperors fighting over ownership of land and people. I was gob-smacked reading the oral histories of working class movements: the Chartists, the Blanketeers, the Suffragists, the Luddites, the Peterloo Massacre and the Tolpuddle Martyrs and to find out how People's History can tell another story.

Ever since then I believed repetition would keep our story buoyant, and one story did lead to the next until we reached the Reunion programme on BBC Radio, which led to the making of the comedy drama film *Misbehaviour* which is now taking our story around the world again, followed by a BBC2 Documentary, *Beauty Queens and Bedlam*.

WHAT HAVE I LEARNT SINCE?

I was invited to talk recently in a local school about our protest. This brought me sharply in touch with young women of today and I heard their concerns about beauty. I spoke about my belief that we all have our own unique inner beauty, but we need to discover it. Of course they wanted to know exactly where it was!

Through talking together we decided that you had to search your inner strength and to believe in yourself in order to develop your own inner beauty with confidence. But we recognized that when we are pitted against each other in competition it is even more important to develop ourselves through our female friendships and to empower each other.

Talking about the Miss World protest at another school with Sue we heard the views and anxieties of young women:

- Social media and the pressure to look good – spending 60% of free time on social media – do something to improve social media, set standards to conform to

- The importance of self-worth

- The need to help one another out and stick together

- Love Island and the hidden meaning behind it?

- Children being exploited in pageants

- We should be judged on inner beauty and personality – looks don't last forever

- Always being sold products – that's the reason we're sold these ideas of beauty

- Female empowerment, need to show a diverse range of body types, including plus-sized models (debate over term plus-sized, should just be models?)

- Power in the media is largely male, need to be women in positions of power

- Our generation have to step up and change things

- Ban beauty pageants!

Since our protest, the beauty world is so much tougher now. I have learnt how we are up against a new monster that threatens us all, the rapidly expanding beauty industry that uses surveillance techniques to harness the data of our very private thoughts and insecurities to enable the creation of new products. This will undermine and control our own creative and unique images of beauty. Now there is so much more at stake as our identities are invaded. Hearing how threatened young women feel today is disturbing and means there is even more to protest about now. With frightening new beauty technology BEAUTIFUL OR UGLY does not matter in the same way as it once had for us. It leaves me feeling even MORE ANGRY now!

Especially learning about the growth of Child Beauty Contests 'Toddlers and Tiaras' in the USA where it is expected that girls will have big hair (including fake hair), flawless makeup, spray tans, flippers (fake teeth), and nail extensions. Children are taught that being over a certain weight isn't considered attractive. For this reason, many young people in the pageant world develop eating disorders such as anorexia nervosa.

In preparation for these beauty pageants, children have their appearances altered by products which objectify them at a very young age. Some pageants encourage contestants to apply heavy makeup to create full lips, long eyelashes, and flushed cheeks, wear high heels and revealing "evening gowns", and do provocative dance steps, poses or facial expressions. wikipedia article accessed 30 August 2020 en.wikipedia.org/wiki/ Child_beauty_pageant, notes 19 and 20

RESISTANCE

In 2013, France banned pageants for children under the age of thirteen years, on the grounds that they promote the "hyper-sexualisation" of minors. France also voted to regulate pageants for children aged 13-15, the first western country to do so.

In Argentina, beauty pageants are now banned in a growing number of municipalities. A long-standing controversy surrounding the values promoted through the contests has escalated in the wake of an alarming number of femicides — the killing of women and girls on account of their gender.

World-wide feminist campaigns have made links between the objectification of women, domestic violence and femicide, so banning beauty contests to combat sexist stereotypes will hopefully continue to grow; outrage over gender-driven violence won't fade.

THERE IS STILL MUCH MORE WORK TO BE DONE!

Carole Vincent A SIXTEEN-YEAR-OLD HIPPY
FEMINIST WHO WENT WITH FRIENDS FROM A PEACE GROUP
TO PROTEST AND DISRUPT THE MISS WORLD CONTEST.
THE GREAT SUCCESS IN GETTING THEIR CAUSE AND VOICE
HEARD SPURRED HER INTO LIFE-LONG ACTIVISM AS A
CAMPAIGNER FOR JUSTICE, PEACE, EQUALITY AND THE
ENVIRONMENT, AND NOW AS A VOLUNTEER GETTING
JUSTICE FOR CLAIMANTS IN AN UNJUST BENEFITS SYSTEM.

In 1970, I was sixteen years old and still at secondary school in Essex. My family had been there for ten years following the slum clearance programme in London's East End. I was a confident child though I felt very out of place in Essex and through my school days.

I was influenced by my dad politically, at a young age, probably around eight or nine years old. He was an electrician, in a Union and had been at the Battle of Cable Street in the autumn of 1936, when Mosley's Fascist Black Shirts tried to march through the East End, only to be met by thousands of people opposing them. My dad took me to Cable Street before having pie and mash at Shadwell. He said, 'As long as you're my daughter, don't ever sit on the fence and don't turn your back on those in need, it could be you one day.'

I had two much older brothers so I was a bit spoiled being the only girl and youngest. I loved music, art, drama and history. I was aware of women, mainly from TV but also from a Women's Peace Group I'd heard about when at a Folk Club, that women were 'burning their bras'! I knew I couldn't do that even if I wanted to because I would be at even greater risk of being teased.

At around this time, having been fed the same size dinners as the adults and a school dinner, being a 'latchkey' kid, after school I'd make a sandwich, if lucky, jam or lemon curd, if not, sugar or mash potato on bread with 'Daddies Sauce'! I started to develop breasts early and spread out a bit too, like my grandmother. I never had body issues, I knew I was loved but I also had long, coarse, thick black, 'frizzy' hair. I got teased and bullied throughout school because of my size and my hair.

I grew up in the 'Swinging Sixties' and tried to follow the civil rights movement in America, with music and fashion all closely-linked. Fashion became a problem when I went to buy clothing; they never had my size, a 16-18 at fourteen years. I was shown to the 'outsize' section and offered crimplene dresses, resembling tents! I hated clothes shopping so my Mum, a seamstress and tailor, got me to design what I wanted and get the material and she'd make things for me. The iconic figures of the day were Twiggy and designer, Mary Quant, with hair by Vidal Sassoon. I could never look like Quant or any of the BIBA fashion models but I could look like Angela Davis and Diana Ross.

By the late sixties, I had a lot of teasing, from boys mainly, they'd say I needed an 'over the shoulder, boulder holder', meaning a bra that was huge or 'let's bring in a crane'. They would refer to me as 'Titsalina bum squeak' which I never understood as I didn't have much of a bottom, it was all breast and belly. I always loved my eyes, hair, breasts and legs, which were like my nan's and mum's.

I had my hair pulled so I plaited it, or cut it as short as I could, without looking like a boy. I was in the school sports teams, rounders, netball, hockey and swimming. I wasn't good at running and track events and on sports days, even in the Juniors, I was teased as I ran the egg and spoon race, I'd hear comments like, 'Oi, Carole, don't let your tits knock it off' or 'Blimey Carole, don't fall over, you'll go blind'. I even had them saying, when I did the sack race, 'Watch out, you'll knock yourself out if you fall over'.

I did feel upset sometimes because it was relentless, and my Mum could see I could easily lose confidence. It was wise of her to tell me that it was those people teasing me that had the problems, and 'sticks and stones will break your bones, but names will never hurt you'. I used that phrase a lot but, names do hurt you and I knew I was lucky having my family.

At thirteen years old I went to my first school disco at a youth centre. I put a bit of make-up on and a skirt and stretch stockings. I suppose I wanted to conform because my friends said they would get a bit 'dolled up'! I've always thought that an odd expression, never knowing what it meant. Was it because dolls always had red lips, rosy pink rouge cheeks, long eye lashes and fine shaped eyebrows? Did it mean women were seen as inanimate playthings? If so, why, who for, where did it come from? I had loads of questions but very few answers!

My mum, dad and I watched TV quite often and even the Miss World Contest as I was growing up. My mum couldn't see why a young woman, and some were only nineteen or twenty, who were wanting to become lawyers and doctors, would also want to parade on TV in expensive gowns and swimsuits. 'What do they get out of it?' she'd say. We did talk about it as we watched.

My dad didn't call it a cattle market but clearly wasn't impressed by 'Beauty Contests'. In fact, in many ways he appeared a bit prudish or old-fashioned in his attitudes. However, I believe having daughters he didn't like women or as he sometimes said, 'these young girls', being 'ogled at', he didn't like the close shots panning up the legs to the crutch in the swimsuit section.

My dad said, 'yes, they're beautiful, but that won't get you through life, my girl.' My mum said, 'they must have money to get all these things like gowns and tiaras', which she knew with thousands of rhinestones must cost a fortune. So her opinion was that, whilst they were students or lawyers or scientists and said they wanted to travel the world and help people, there was a vanity and class element, because they had the money to pursue it.

It made me think more about whether a working-class woman could be part of it. I also said, 'well, you don't have men's beauty contests.' My dad referred to Mr Universe, but saw that as more about strength, though we did agree that the men entering were all groomed and handsome and oiled up with skimpy Speedos so, was it the same?

I thought about the male and female form shown off and paraded through history and wondered what the Greeks or Romans must have thought.

I had been attending the East Hertfordshire Women's Peace Group when I could and was going to the Folk Club often. I also ran a junior Drama Group at the local theatre and met 'hippy' types like myself. We would chat about music and women's liberation, though I think it was called women's rights, rights to contraception and choices around our bodies, equal pay if you do the same job as a man, how roles are depicted in plays and on TV, for example women tied to the kitchen sink and in subservient roles or seen as nagging wives and comedic figures to be ridiculed!

This was bloody great, meeting like-minded people; I was going on anti-apartheid demos and also looking at having a career doing something other than being a 'housewife'. Nothing wrong with being able to run a home, but plenty wrong with gender defined roles. I and my brothers were expected to do cooking, cleaning, decorating, changing a plug and so on. I was lucky, but my friends were sometimes cooking and cleaning and 'waiting on' their male siblings and dads, who went to the pub or watched football, whilst the girls and women did all the domestic chores.

I met a woman a bit older than me at the Folk Club, her name was Lizzie. We struck up a conversation and the subject turned from music to politics and other issues like the Vietnam War and women's liberation and she asked if I would be interested in joining them on an 'action'. I was excited and said 'yes' but couldn't go on the date given so I gave her my phone number in case anything else cropped up. I kept reading about the women's movement in the US, then one evening my mum answered the phone. It was late autumn in 1970 and it was Lizzie.

I didn't want my mum to know what I was doing as she may have been worried, but she overheard my conversation when I said 'Oh, yeah, I'll come.' She asked, 'What's that for? It sounds exciting!' I told her about it. I thought it would be an adventure and I was both anxious and excited. Lizzie had told me that her women's group were going to do a direct action. I was told that someone had dropped out of the group last minute and they needed someone to step in. I asked what it was and she said, 'you just need to get a ticket for the underground into London; it's the Miss World Contest'. I exclaimed, 'Oh, I can't stand that' to which she replied, 'That's why we asked you'. She said, 'Come in all your finery.'

Blue Psychadelic Top ⟶

Purple Loons Velvet

Knee-high Platform Boots

We were to meet and travel by underground from Epping to the Albert Hall and I knew it was posh but had never been. I was asked to take some food and drink for the journey, I said I didn't have any money but Lizzie told me tickets were taken

'Me in my finery' Drawing by Carole Vincent

care of. My Mum made me this blue 'psychedelic' patterned top with flowing sleeves and I wore loons, and kinky boots with patent platforms, all the rage, and my black, smoky BIBA eyeliner.

We met and travelled to London and talked about what we'd be doing. I'd been told not to tell anyone, but I told my mum and she slipped me a whole £10 note as I left, and said, 'Don't get arrested!' Lizzie had got a banner folded under her long coat and she and the other women had got poles to put the banner on, under their coats.

I was told that when the word was given, we would unfurl the banner and make some noise. We arrived at the Albert Hall and I was excited and nervous but very committed to the cause of women being liberated and getting more power and rights, equality in lots of areas really. However, arriving, I expected there to be a huge queue and to stand for ages and that we'd get arrested by security. There was hardly any security, the queue we were in was moving quickly and we were in and seated in a line, in the middle of the second tier.

We were passed a card as we sat down, it read: when Lizzie gives the order, to stand and unfurl the banner and shout, 'We object, we're not objects!'. It started, the momentary silence was broken when people clapped and Bob Hope swaggered onto the stage. I thought, What's he doing here, he's like a spare part?!

Lizzie was getting the banner from under her long coat and passing it along the row, two women sitting to the left and right were fiddling with the sticks in the banner. The people in the row in front were telling us, 'Shush, shush', 'Stop fidgeting'. The word came as I heard commotion from nearer the stage area, a sort of clanging sound and lots more women shouting. I'm not sure what happened to Bob Hope, nor did I care! We'd done it, we were up on our feet chanting and shouting, 'We object, we're not objects, our bodies, our own,' repeated until security came to try to get us. There was chaos and not enough security; they were mainly near the women below us.

We shuffled from our seats to escape, about eight women were pulling the banner left and right, I'd dropped it to get out. I tried to find the exit and someone asked me where it was, I told them, I wasn't 'one of them', meaning the protesters and joined the toilet queue. Once in the toilet, I was calling my accomplices names. I got no response but had to get out as security was looking for us and I saw three of my friends being hauled out. I was approached but told them I wasn't a protester; I was just going to the toilet. My heart was pounding and I turned to the opposite direction, found the stairs and 'legged it' out.

 My feet were killing me and my legs shaking. There were loads of police outside and a big van, a 'Black Maria'. Women were still shouting. We had made a plan not to have ID on us and to meet at the underground if we weren't arrested. There were women leaving the auditorium and I followed until I got to the underground. I met just one of the women I went with, and we waited only a short time before leaving for fear of missing the last bus at Epping. I ate my sandwiches, hardly said a word and got the last but one bus home safely.

I got home, my parents had been watching it and my dad had said, 'What's all the fuss about' and mum had said to my dad, 'How did they even get in there?,' 'I hope she hasn't got arrested!' Two of our friends got arrested for breach of the peace, the other was let go that night. I never did get to the trial but I recall it being in the papers that some women were convicted! They were my heroines after that.

The adrenalin was marvellous and I was fired up for some more action, I played all the protest songs I could find on my record player, from Joan Baez to Bob Dylan. It was such a brilliant achievement and I've continued to be an activist and campaigner all my life. I've been a Union member and Shop Steward and led and been on picket lines fighting for justice.

I became more interested in the suffrage movement, the Bryant and May Match strike, anti-racism and anti-fascism. Along with becoming a member of the Campaign for Nuclear Disarmament, I've continued my anti-war activity, joining Stop the War Coalition following the invasion of Iraq, anti-nuclear power and Trident, along with a fight against the Arms Trade, and I continue to be driven politically.

I am a committed socialist, a mother, grandmother and great grandmother, and I suppose having counted George Orwell amongst my favourite authors, I had Big Brother watching me for 94 days when I became the oldest civilian finalist in the Big Brother House in 2007.

Carole Vincent and children at Greenham Common

Carole de Jong AN ARTIST WHO
DEMONSTRATED OUTSIDE THE MISS WORLD CONTEST
IN 1970 AND THE TRIAL OF THE PROTESTERS, AND
HASN'T STOPPED PROTESTING SINCE

In the late '60s I was having a great time! An artist and sculptor,
I was in the Labour party and around the European Communist
party. I was very active against the Vietnam War – demonstrating
and marching – but women's views weren't heard.

When the women's movement started we thought 'Thank God!' I went
to the Oxford Women's Conference in 1970, then the Birmingham
conference later, and was a member of the second women's group
that started in London, the Belsize Lane Group . The group grew and
grew then divided into three groups, I'm still in touch with half the
women. We were reading everything we could get our hands on: it all
started with Betty Friedan for me. *The Feminine Mystique*, then *The
Female Eunuch* (Germaine Greer) and Erica Jong's *Fear of Flying*.
The stuff we had been puzzling about, suddenly everyone was saying
the same thing, it was enlightening! We wrote an edition of *Shrew*
(the Women's Liberation Workshop newsletter) on The Family, and
read *Spare Rib*. Some of our writing was so witty . .

I was part of the Miss World demonstration outside the Albert Hall,
wearing a duffle coat (as always). We weren't protesting against
the contestants, but about how women were being perceived. The
contest was horrible, a cattle market. It's difficult to recall how we
felt, it wasn't life and death, but we wanted the men to do things
differently. They had to be stupid to judge women by their looks
rather than their skills or intellect. The judges asked such patronising

questions! Some of us had banners saying 'Misrepresented', Misinformed', etc. I can't remember much more than that, it was cold and dark, but it was kind of enjoyable – it felt joyous. And why not? There was so much seriousness around.

The action made a lot of people think. It had an impact, but not on a grand scale. Tragic that the contest is still going on...

I was outside the trial demonstrating with my friend Val, and there's a lovely photo to prove it, but can't remember much about it.

I was on the ad-hoc organising committee for the International Women's Day march in 1971, and a steward. Our group was very active around the Night Cleaners strike, and I started to work in film, as well as teaching ceramics at Camden Adult Institute.

Carole and Val outside Bow Street Magistrate's Court
London, February 1971: Photo © Sally Fraser

I created the photo on the front of *The Body Politic*, a collection of women's liberation writings which included 'Women and the Family' from the Oxford Women's Conference in 1970 and a chapter on the Miss World demonstration (ed. Michelene Wandor, 1972).

When my son started at the Children's Community Centre in Dartmouth Park Hill, a community nursery set up and run by women in the area, we all did a day a week. At the beginning of the 70s, it was possible to do so much. There was a good Labour government, then Thatcher came!

In the 80s I was part of the 'Embrace the Base' action at the Greenham Common women's peace camp in 1982, and worked on *The Greenham Factor*, a publication about the peace camp that eventually led to the removal of the cruise missiles that the US had based there.

I marched for the miners, left the Labour party over the Iraq war, joined again a couple of years ago. We demonstrated against Bush and now against Trump – the world has gone mad!

Last year we had an exhibition at the Holborn Library to commemorate the suffragettes 100 years on – and it included some of my art.

Now I'm feeling a bit isolated, there's a terrible division between the rich and the poor, people going to food banks – in our country! Since Thatcher and the Me generation it's a total disaster. It's going to get worse if Brexit goes ahead. I'm totally disillusioned and at a loss about how people don't seem to care. People stabbed to death on the street (one right outside my door), sleeping rough – while rich people get huge bonuses.

But I'm not giving up!

Poster Workshop.

Jenny Fortune's STORY STARTED IN CROYDON, DAUGHTER OF A CAR DEALER WITH OLD FASHIONED IDEAS ABOUT A WOMAN'S PLACE. IT TAKES US THROUGH A REVOLUTIONARY AWAKENING AT ESSEX UNIVERSITY, IN A VAN LOAD OF WOMEN DRIVING TO THE MISS WORLD PROTEST ' FIRED UP WITH DISGUST, BRAVADO AND ANXIETY' THROUGH TO SQUATTING IN EAST LONDON AND WORKING AS AN ARCHITECT IN SHEFFIELD.

I squeezed with seven others into a tiny van and set off from Essex for the Miss World Competition of 1970, collecting the entrance tickets, smoke bombs, football rattles and leaflets for the event from a house in London on the way. The eight of us were an assemblage of students and lecturers' wives at one of the new universities (Essex) of the '60s, part of the massive expansion that gave women access to a university education for the first time. We had formed a Women's Liberation group after hearing Sheila Rowbotham speak at the first UK women's liberation meeting at the Essex Revolutionary Festival in 1969 and the Oxford Women's Conference of 1970.

My first reaction to hearing about the ideas of Women's Liberation had been dismay – 'But that would lead to families breaking up!' it took a while for the penny to drop. To think about why my own family had already broken up. After years of total financial dependence on my father, whilst bringing up a family of six children, my mother had finally found a way of earning her own income and had left my father in 1968, in anticipation of the divorce laws liberalising in 1969.

I embarked on an exploratory venture into feminist literature: *The*

Sheila Rowbotham, foreground right, at Women's Liberation Conference, 1970

Female Eunuch, The Second Sex, The Longest Revolution, Sexual Politics. I had undoubtedly benefited from going to a girl's grammar school in Croydon, which I suspect attracted particularly progressive and feminist-minded teachers, now I look back at what we studied. So I was already prepped to be an independent thinker. The leather jacketed, smoked-filled egotistical bombast of the university male left had left me fairly puzzled and made me feel inadequate. And so the ideas I heard at the Women's Liberation conference, like the paper on *Women and the family* by Jan Williams and Hazel Twort, were like the sun appearing from behind the clouds. The confidence and shining exuberance of the speakers and all the women at the conference made me feel that I was entering a brave new world.

It all gave me permission to talk about my own life and experience again, but through a totally different political lens. Consciousness-raising helped me in the first uncertain steps of trusting other women enough to voice inner uncertainties. It took a long time to be able to understand myself through these writings and discussions, to see how my own persona was shaped by a male-defined world. At the same time 'Free Love' in the after-glow of the hippy summer of love of 1968 was in full force in the universities, aided by copious supplies of drugs and alcohol; contraception clinics had just opened, and we were fully expected to be sexually available to just about anybody.

The ensuing clash of inner and outer identities must have found its perfect outlet in anger about the Miss World contest. Those women stiffened and painted by male shapers, represented all that we were escaping from and wanted to change. An essential driver of my attraction to feminism was that of having control over my own body; I wanted to enjoy the beauty and sexuality of my body without feeling it was there primarily for male enjoyment and the male eye of approval. My transition from enjoying my life as a tomboy, climbing trees and playing football with my three older brothers, to young woman, had been all about my body. As an eleven-year-old I had prided myself on having short hair, wearing scruffy clothes and loving classical music: a classic nerd. I remember distinctly sitting and watching my three years older sister talking make-up and nail varnish with a friend, knowing that was something I never wanted to do – or be. But, probably no more than a year later, I was agonising about having no breasts or periods and wondering whether there was something wrong with me. I remember the relief when I eventually started bleeding and disbelief at the lumpy smelly pads I had to start wearing, and struggles in the bathroom with tampons, the humiliation of not being able to get it in.

Women's Street Theatre Trafalgar Square. Women's march, 1971: Photo © Sally Fraser.

I have such a strong memory of becoming aware of the male gaze — it seemed to just arrive one day, and I remember an overwhelming sense of self-consciousness and, yes, power. In the safety of the consciousness-raising group I explored the meaning of the male gaze and the way I had adapted myself to its requirements, to the required look and behaviour of a potential 'girlfriend'. The patriarchal gaze, legitimised by the Miss World contest, blocked me from developing my identity and self-determination as I wanted. The Miss World spectacle embodied all this on live TV and this was good enough for me to squeeze into that van to stop it. I had no idea, but this was to be the turning point of my life; by taking action I was symbolically freeing myself from those constraints.

So we queued up outside the Albert Hall with our bags, rattles and bundles concealed under our dubious glamour (an assemblage of begged, borrowed and stolen coats and dresses). We knew the plan was to bring the contest to a complete halt, and that two of the women would give the signal to start at some point before the crowning of Miss World. We wanted to make it absolutely clear that our attack was against the whole sleazy premise of the spectacle, not the contestants themselves. The best moment was considered to be during Bob Hope's set. We had watched his show the previous year when he took Miss World 1969 to entertain the US troops in Vietnam. His cynical disdain for those sweating and disorientated young lads, set up as fodder for the US war machine had made me feel distressed and sick; these were boys like my brothers. The wheeling out of puppet doll Eva Rueber-Staeir whose sole utterance was 'I'm only a woman', her beauty queen persona somehow designed to show those confused boys that really they were MEN, there to desire and protect the existence of that simulacrum of femininity. Her deceitful stick-doll fragility intended to compensate for the slaughter of those young bodies, their self-esteem and mental health. All compounded by Bob Hope's sneering put-down quips about the draft 'I know you're all thrilled about the new draft lottery' and his final quip about Eve Rueber-Staeir on asking for her vital statistics: 'well you've sold me – where does a civilian go to RE up?', referring to the soldiers' 'Rest and Relaxation' time with prostitutes in Saigon.

We had seats on the top balcony with an awe-inspiring view of the glamorous spectacle. The Lionel Blair dancers

From Why Miss World? pamphlet, 1971:
Cartoon Jenny Fortune.

flew around the stage culminating in a rousing chorus of 'She...who was going to win the crown' (the crown itself being a slight wonky looking tinsel affair that had always sat badly on the winners head), and so began the interminable boredom of Phase 1: dolls stood on the mantelpiece in national dress, parading forward one by one. We amused ourselves with counting the number of countries (most of them) whose national female role model was ... the milkmaid. A little hanky-panky in the stable, eh, eh? *A leetle roll in ze hay?*

The 'girls' are chivvied away after the Phase Two bum display, to parade back again for Phase Three, the glam evening dress. What girl wouldn't want to parade her beauty in an absolutely fabulous dress? I can't help eyeing the dresses appreciatively. They glide forward, one by one – this is the highlight of the event, twirling, floating, glittering – full of flounces, frills and head dresses.

'Is it me, or have they all got Twiggy make-up on?' I ask Val, sitting to one side of me tapping her fingers with impatience. Twiggy was the super-model of the day. Her look was startlingly different from the ideal of female beauty up until then: women of poise and voluptuousness, expressing an air of upper-class nonchalance, born to wear clothes that expressed an unaffordable price tag. Twiggy was as thin as a stick, looked about twelve years old, and showcased skimpy clothes (the miniskirt) in awkward gangly, childlike poses.

Her trademark look was over-enlarged eyes, emphasized by gigantic eyelashes that looked as though tarantula spiders had taken over her face (I can hear my grandfather's disapproving voice here). Each Miss World contestant sported similar eyelashes and doll-like facial make-up, beneath a Marie-Antoinette style hairdo of the time, bouffant and lacquered, curled and back-combed and piled high, all stiff as a board. The eyeshadow was bright blue (Liz Taylor in *Cleopatra*), the eyebrows highly arched (ditto). The look denoted a struggle between the '50s womanly curviness appropriate to the stay-at-home housewife and mother, the desire for glamour and 'queenliness' epitomised by Liz Taylor, and the emerging '60s ambition and availability of the teenage girl, aspiring to be independent and a 'career girl'. Surely this look had been concocted by make-up artists who appreciated little about female beauty, and were struggling to express both the traditional and modern concepts of femininity that were jostling for supremacy in the male-dominated fashion and media world. The resulting look they imposed on those lovely faces was one of a highly painted, immobilised and scared-looking doll.

The Hollywood Star arrived on the stage – Bob Hope, star of such greats as *My Favourite Blonde, My Favourite Brunette, Call Me Paleface, Call Me Bwana, The Road to Zanzibar.* 'They couldn't have found anyone more appropriate' snarled Zena, sitting the other side of me, 'but hey, isn't he looking a bit...er...pale?'

Bob Hope was indeed looking a bit white around the gills. Could it be that hosting this event was a bit of a comedown for him, a bit sleazy for a star of Hollywood fame? Or maybe he had noticed the counterculture rumbling outside, he had heard that the BBC van had been blown up the night before. He seemed to be repeatedly looking over his shoulder furtively – or was that his style? Was he anticipating a booing as soon as he hit the stage? There was a slight dramatic pause, a sense that the audience in the tiered temple of royalty and pomp was sniffing the air, testing the atmosphere. Was that an impatient rustle over there? Was that an odour that floated free from an un-deodorised and hairy armpit?

'Moooo' said Bob Hope, followed by a slight flinch and look over the shoulder 'Welcome to the cattle market'. Game on, I thought, now it's going to start. But only a scatter of uncomfortable laughter. A series of very flat jokes followed. 'Can't get my wife to wear a cloth coat' (What was a cloth coat? I wondered in incomprehension). He resorted to his paean to the US invasion of Vietnam and his own vital role in parading out Miss World to 'make the troops feel hot'. Our rage must have been flowing over that balcony, but still nothing happened, nothing amiss, nobody noticing we weren't your typical audience members.

Bob Hope droned on and on, making no pretence of reading his jokes out directly from the flipchart held in front of him, someone struggling to turn the pages fast enough to keep up with him. I hissed to the others 'They've chickened out – the moment has passed'. We sank back into our seats, deflated. The prospect of returning to Essex in that damn van, having done nothing except watch the interminable boredom of the dispiriting show. Who did we think we were anyway – what made us believe we were courageous enough to shatter the spectacle?

But below the droning on of the comic a different sound began. A faint grind-rattle, grind-rattle – what was it? We had expected whistles, hoots and shouts – what was this subdued sound? Grind- rattle, on and on – it slowly picked up a rhythm, gained in volume. The grand hall held its breath. The air changed, a breeze wafted through the tiers as people turned around to make out where the sound was coming from. A piece of paper floated down from above. Suddenly a shriek, 'Stop the cattle market', a shrill whistle, another shout, 'We're not beautiful, we're not ugly, we're angry!' turned into a chant. Hoots, whistles, football rattles – people were running towards the stage where Bob Hope cowered, holding banners, 'Women's Liberation Now!'.

'This is it girls, we're on!' someone yelled, and we emptied our bags

'Essex girls hit the spot'
Cartoon Jenny Fortune 2020.

of flour and sheaves of leaflets over the balcony, blew our whistles and party kazoos. The Albert Hall in front of us transformed into a sublime storm of flour, leaflets, women running around dodging the bouncers, shouting out loud. From balconies all around the hall our flour floated in clouds onto the bejewelled spectators below, the leaflets rained down. How glorious – we'd done it! The whole thing ground to a complete halt. The stage emptied, Bob Hope tried to run for it, Julia Morley grabbed his ankle to stop him, the orchestra ducked, the audience gasped.

It was all so much better than we had hoped would be possible – the eight of us whooped and shouted in exhilaration – delighted at the sight of Bob Hope running for cover. We had a panoramic of the whole thing. I had never been so excited in my life. I didn't want it to stop and pulled out one of the toy smoke bombs and struggled to get the cigarette lighter to catch the tiny wick, determined to make my final gesture. I hadn't noticed in my intense concentration that the others had decided to quietly beat a retreat 'Come on Jenny we're going' they hissed. I felt a heavy hand on my shoulder, caught a navy-blue jacket with shiny buttons out of the corner of my eye. Where was everybody – who was this?

'Come on you, out with you.' Two burly policemen carried me out and down the stairs out of the hall and into a waiting police van. I was on my own. None of us had thought about the possibility of being arrested. The plan was to slip away unnoticed, which the others had executed successfully, on their way back to Essex no doubt.

From Why Miss World? pamphlet, 1971, Cartoon Jenny Fortune.

I was put in a police cell, I hadn't a clue where. The adrenaline was dissipating quickly. I was left to contemplate my crime. The cell was small and unheated on that November night – a bench seat along one side with peeling green paint, a wall of iron bars with a gate opposite me. The kind of prison cell a drunkard is thrown into, the gangster or innocent hero in cowboy films. I felt numb and couldn't quite work out the reality of what had happened to me. After a couple of hours, two gentlemen were ushered into my cell, clad in beige belted raincoats and brown trilby hats. One of them introduced himself to me as Inspector Habershon of M15 – the Bomb Squad. He is portly with partly balding black hair and moustache. He makes me think of Stan Laurel of Laurel & Hardy. I don't consider him a frightening figure of authority, and he doesn't seem to consider me a serious contender for being a terrorist bomber. Long silences ensue after he has asked me if I had anything to do with the bomb under the BBC van the night before, to which I answer that we were furious with whoever it was, that the Women's Liberation Movement had nothing to do with such upstaging tactics, probably by a bunch of early mansplaining anarchists. Inspector Habershon seemed convinced by my squeaky indignation and retreated with a disappointed sigh, I was obviously not who he was looking for.

It turned out five of us had been arrested. The work began to prepare for the trial. The next few days were a roller coaster of emotions. The world had seen the televised spectacle of constructed female competition shattered – publicly, emphatically, joyously – and I was, improbably, one of the figureheads of this. Bob Hope's response had been 'these people....must be on some kind of dope' (which possibly confirmed my family's suspicions), followed up by a very sinister quip 'sooner or later these people have to get paid off... you know – there's somebody up there takes care of these things'.

We were mainly vilified by the press, my family did not know what to make of me – their disapproval lightened somewhat by my oldest brother, a veteran of the Campaign for Nuclear Disarmament, The Committee of 100, the Aldermaston march who had been arrested on the anti-Vietnam War demo outside the US embassy, saying 'Good on you'.

But to all those around the five of us, we were heroines. The next Women's Liberation Workshop meeting decided that we were to defend ourselves in court. The atmosphere in that meeting was triumphant – full of strong and talented women – writers, artists, film-makers, academics, a smattering of Trade Unionists and Labour Party members. Those women were on the cusp of breaking through into the mainstream and making their voices heard. It was agreed that we were to reject the charges and the legitimacy of the court, turn the tables and put the patriarchal legal system on trial instead.

Who me? I was twenty, in my first year at university, barely left home. The acclaim and euphoria in being a heroine turned cold, clammy and frightening. My closest friends in the London house, Sue and Jo, were preoccupied with childbirth. Sue had given birth to Kelly a few days after the demonstration, and Jo (who would be on trial with me) was five months pregnant and trying sort out her relationship with the father. I was on my own to make this decision. I went to the local park, sat in an isolated corner on a cold December afternoon and entered the most challenging period of my life up until then.

The choice was clear: play safe as my family assumed I would, buy a respectable coat and get a conventional lawyer to explain what a nice girl I really was and how I had been led astray by a bunch of hippies and hadn't really meant it 'your honour'. Go back to university and continue into a career.

Or: join the revolution, be a public spokeswoman for the Women's Liberation Movement, put the case coherently for why we had done it, challenge the magistrate and the police on their values.

Hours ticked by on that cold stone bench. My future was in these transforming networks which the friends I was on trial with were part of; we were spread around the world – young Americans who refused to go to fight in Vietnam; Irish women who came to stay for a few weeks in order to secure an abortion; Spanish, Portuguese, Greek and Latin-American exiles from dictatorships – we were looking after each other. Home felt like the communal house that sheltered me whilst I was making my mind up.

Reader – I decided to defend myself, join the revolution and leave university.

The next few weeks were spent organising our act. We got advice from a radical set of lawyers who were helping two of the Mangrove 9 defend themselves as a result of a police raid on an Afro-Caribbean restaurant in Notting Hill Gate.

My experience of the trial proved to be transformative, from the first moment of walking into Bow Street court through crowds of supporters who were fronted by the Gay Liberation Front street theatre, clothed in their flashing breasts and peacock outfits.

'Their case opened at Bow Street Magistrate's Court on 4th February 1971. GLF Street Theatre received a request from Women's Liberation to perform outside the court on the first morning of the trial in order to show support and draw attention to their campaign against Mecca and the Miss World Contest. At last, *Street Theatre* had a real issue to work on, and with the top down duo of Winter and Wakeling out of the way, the Think In demand that we work collectively was put into practice. Everyone's ideas for this performance were discussed, and out of them developed The Miss Trial Competition, with contestants named Miss Judged, Miss Used, Miss Taken, Miss Behaved, Miss Conception and Miss Understood who were interviewed by a compere and told the story from the protestors' point of view. We agreed that we would not have a director, and that we would ad lib rather than having a script; we wanted to be spontaneous and 'in the moment'. Neon Edsel and I appeared wearing Felliniesque swimwear with padded bosoms and surrealist painted blue eyes for nipples'. Stuart Feather, *Blowing the Lid: Gay Liberation, Sexual Revolution and Radical Queens*, Pub: Zero books, 2016.

GLF Theatre outside Bow Street Court, London, February 1971: Cartoon Jenny Fortune 2020.

With the support of the (mainly) women in the gallery I found my voice. I found my voice was confident and articulate, I found the words (with the help of Jo and Kate) to explain why we had done it, challenge the presumptions of the male establishment and law. We spent every day and night after leaving the courtroom planning our speeches and questions of witnesses. With advice from Sally Alexander's barrister, we served subpoenas on Bob Hope and Eric Morley (both avoided coming to court). We decided to call the magistrate 'Daddy' throughout.

'Magistrate Geraint Evans breaks out in a sweat'. From Why Miss World? pamphlet 1971:
Cartoon Jenny Fortune.

4 Miss World defendants held in custody

By FLORENCE KEYWORTH

THERE WERE angry scenes at the Bow Street, London, hearing of the Miss World case yesterday and at the end of the day all four defendants were remanded in custody until today.

The first scene occurred when police seized hold of Miss Jo Robinson, 28, who is one of four defendants who went to the Miss World contest at the Albert Hall on November 20 to stop the show.

She had asked permission to leave the court to go to the toilet and on her return she put her head through the court doorway and shouted: "A witness is being held on the stairs outside here and is being questioned by the police. We want a solicitor."

When police tried to drag Miss Robinson inside the court she refused to come shouting: "I won't come in until we have a solicitor."

ALL SHOUTING

The three other defendants, Catherine McLean, 20, Sally Alexander, 27, and Jennifer Fortune, 21, were all shouting their protests from the dock as the magistrate adjourned the case for five minutes.

When Miss Nina Stanger, defending, had finished examining Miss Alexander, Miss Fortune jumped up in the dock and said she too wished to question her. Despite orders from the magistrate, Mr. Geraint Rees, that he would not allow this, Miss Alexander answered some of Miss Fortune's questions.

"What do you think of the magistrate?" asked Miss Fortune. "He is a symbol of authority. He is here to preserve the status quo," replied Miss Alexander.

All the defendants protested together when the magistrate refused their request that Mr. Eric Morley, chief of the Mecca organisation, which held the Miss World contest, should be subpoenaed as a witness.

NOT RENEWED

The clerk told the court that Mr. Morley had been asked to appear on December 22 and that the summons had not been renewed.

There were more stormy scenes when Miss Fortune and her fellow defendants later protested because she was not allowed to call all the witnesses she wished.

The magistrate ordered that all four girls should be held in custody until the case resumes at 2 p.m. today.

There will be a demonstration outside the court at 1.30 p.m.

Following incidents outside the court, Sue Finch, a witness who gave evidence at an earlier hearing, was arrested and charged with assault on the police.

Three other supporters, Jane Grant, Sarah Martin and Sarah Wilson, were, it was understood, taken to Barnet police station for

One of the Women's Liberation supporters who picketed the Miss World trial in London yesterday. Her banner shows the ... of the movement.

Magistrate fines Alb Hall 'bomb' throwe

By FLORENCE KEYWORTH

THE four young women who demonstrated at the Miss World Contest in the Albert Hall last November were fined sums of £10 or £20 with £5 costs at Bow Street, London, yesterday.

Smoke bombs, bags of flour and tomatoes were all thrown during the contest which the defendants have described as "insulting to women." They have described the organisers of the show as "the Mecca pimps."

Miss Jennifer Fortune, 21, who was arrested in the Albert Hall while, according to police evidence, she was attempting to light a smoke bomb, was fined £10 for threatening behaviour.

NOT THE FIRST

"We are not the first women who have challenged society and the way it treats us and we are not going to be the last," she said before being sentenced.

Miss Sally Alexander, 27, who had told the court that she ran down the aisle at the Albert Hall

phone, was fined ... threatening behaviour.

A charge against he ... ing a police officer ... missed.

She was represent Nina Stanger who tol "The females being the Albert Hall was as saleable commod ...

"That is abhorre ... women, and possibly ... ber of men. This ...

★ continued o

DECIMAL

Points to watch Monday. Decimalists SEE PAGE ...

Holidays

Britain's 200,000 ... yesterday put in a c ... weeks annual hol ... double overtime ra ...

Four 'Miss World' protesters fined

★ *continued from p. 1*

ing a police officer was dismissed.

She was represented by Miss Nina Stanger who told the court: "The females being displayed at the Albert Hall were displayed as saleable commodities.

"That is abhorrent to many women, and possibly a large number of men. This display in its nature was likely to incite people to want to demonstrate against it.

Miss Jo Robinson, 28, was fined £10 for insulting behaviour and £10 for throwing a missile. Her offences were said to have taken place outside the Cafe de Paris to which the Miss World contestants were taken after the Albert Hall show.

Miss Catherine McLean, 20, who was arrested at the same time, was also fined £10 on each of two similar charges. All the girls were ordered to pay £5 costs and were bound over to keep the peace for two years.

Charges against all of them of possessing offensive weapons were dismissed by the magistrate, Mr. Geraint Rees.

MY FREEDOM

He said he was satisfied that the smoke bombs were not made or adapted for causing injury to the person. They could cause discomfort and if they fell in a crowd they could cause alarm but they could not be described as offensive weapons.

"I accept that these defendants met beforehand and planned to disrupt these proceedings of the Miss World contest in ways short of causing injury or violence. I accept that," he said.

Miss Fortune told him: "That contest was a threat to my freedom as a woman. I want freedom to determine my own life, my work, my appearance. The contest was symptomatic of the way we are exploited as women.

"We are exploited in our jobs where we are paid less, in the home where we are frustrated with boring housework, in the way we are treated as sexual objects."

Miss Robinson declared: "It is said we were insulting. I feel insulted every day of my life by advertisements in which women are used and objectified."

But the magistrate said the Miss World contest was a perfectly lawful function attended by hundreds if not thousands of perfectly ordinary reasonable people.

"The law entitles them to go there and will protect them when they go there. The defendants must recognise that and if they don't they must face the consequences," he said.

After the case concluded it was stated on behalf of three of the defendants that while in custody certain questions had been put to them in connection with "far more sensational matters."

There might be a likelihood of arrest and detention for questioning by the police, said counsel who appeared briefly on their behalf just before the court rose.

[...] and I know what it feels like to be judged and scrutinised every day when I am walking down the street.

"I saw women being forced to compete with each other and being judged by men. I felt for them. I had no intention of hurting them or attacking them in any way.

Aimed at Bob Hope

"We did not throw anything on to the stage when the contestants were there. We threw missiles on the stage when Bob Hope was speaking.

"In the same way we threw nothing when the Miss World contestants were going into the Cafe de Paris. This was a conscious decision. We regard these contestants as unfortunate victims of the male capitalist system."

The system, she said, made money by persuading women to buy goods such as false eyelashes. "We are sick of all this line about beauty. We are not beautiful and we are not ugly. It is a big capitalist con."

Miss McLean was one of four defendants appearing on charges [...] the "Mecca pimps."

Turning to the magistrate she explained: "The Mecca pimps are the men who are making all the money out of these contests."

Later she herself had thrown a bag of flour. She said that at the police station after her arrest the police were "incredibly rude" and also kept waking up the defendants throughout the night, every 20 minutes, or so, to try to get them to make statements.

"They tried to intimidate us by telling us stories. They said they had witnesses from the crowd when they had no witnesses from the crowd," she said.

Charges against a fifth defendant, Miss Mair Twissell, who was said to have used insulting words, were dismissed by the magistrate, Mr. Geraint Rees.

No evidence

PC Graham Keen said Miss Twissell was with some demonstrators outside the Albert Hall, and while the audience were leaving she thrust her arm between himself and another policeman and shouted "Fuck off" at a woman in the audience.

He had then arrested her.

Questioned by Miss Nina Stanger, defending, he agreed that a woman in the audience had shouted something to the demonstrators and Miss Twissell had shouted back in reply.

Miss Stanger later submitted that there was no evidence that a breach of the peace was likely to be occasioned. Miss Twissell had been charged with using indecent language, but Miss Stanger submitted that the expression was not indecent.

"It may be immodest but that is a question of taste, not of law," she said. Applause greeted the magistrate's dismissal of the summonses against Miss Twissell.

Accused of bias

Miss Fortune submitted vehemently from the dock that the magistrate was biased. "You are the representative of a legal system which exists to defend property, which depends on a family structure which oppresses women" she said.

"You have been behaving like an irascible old schoolmaster. I have been treated as a school girl and I refuse to be called impertinent."

The defendants called five

Pulled out

Earlier evidence was given about Pc Colin Burke who had been on duty at the Albert Hall during the Miss World contest.

He said he had been sitting immediately behind Miss Fortune in the balcony and had seen her try to light a small cylindrical object. He leant over, seized hold of her left hand and pulled her out of her seat.

He denied he was prejudiced against women, but Miss Robinson asked him: "Are you sure you don't regard them as inferior? How is it that you laughed when you were asked the question the first time?" At this Mr. Rees declared: "Let us get down to the reality of the case."

"This is the reality," said all five defendants.

We scrutinised the list of prosecution witnesses and planned our questions to challenge the policemen who had arrested us to explain their relationships with their wives and their domestic arrangements, 'Who washes your socks?' Jo, who was by then six months pregnant, discovered that a pregnant woman on trial had the right to go to the toilet as often as she needed. This was used as a ruse whenever we felt we needed to confer, or simply have a break and meet up with our supporters outside the courtroom. We were put in Holloway for one night, to teach us a lesson – and this was a lesson in what life is like for women in prison. Stripped, sanitised with disinfectant, locked alone in a tiny cell for hours, listening to the cat-calls and songs floating through the bars, wondering whether I was going to be left in prison for the next six months and what on earth I was going to do for the rest of my life after this; the isolation was salutary after the euphoria of the common strength between the five of us and our supporters.

We emerged from Holloway chastened, but greeted and celebrated by our supporters. The experience of defending myself was so profoundly surprising and empowering that I emerged from the trial feeling like a different woman. I had overcome my fear and found that a night in Holloway was the worst that could happen to me – I never looked back.

One of the first things we did was produce a women's newspaper.

Facing page >
From **Women's Newspaper** Issue 1, 1971:
Cover cartoon Jenny Fortune.

WOMEN'S NEWSPAPER

no 1. march 6th. 1971

3p

I flew, not fell. The feminist movement took me into squatting, childcare, working in a factory, learning to plumb and wire a house, fix a car and motor bike engine.

Women's Liberation march 1973 poster: Jenny Fortune 1973.

Together with men, if we had any in our lives, we ran food co-ops, children's nurseries and housed single mothers.

Women's Liberation march 1973 poster: Jenny Fortune 1973.

I read Marx and started to work out how it explained the world, but in relation to my own experience. I learnt about my body, what pleased me sexually and gave me an orgasm. Squatting rows of houses together in abandoned East London streets gave me a sense of neighbourhood and belonging.

Poster Workshop.

The Women's Liberation Movement was extraordinary. We decided what we wanted to do – whether it was to build a house or examine our own vaginas and decide whether to have a child or not – and simply went ahead and taught ourselves and each other how to do it. The essence of the movement was mutual empowerment and self-determination, with the emphasis on supporting each other, and that changed the world.

Women's Liberation March, London, 6 March 1971. Photo © Sally Fraser.

How has this made me what I am today? It undoubtedly gave me the confidence to decide to train to be an architect at the age of thirty and to be gainfully employed for thirty-five years. It gave me a clear political perspective and moral compass in relation to how I practised and taught (and often got me into trouble at work). Being financially independent has been a crucial pillar of my life, no doubt informed by seeing what my mother went through. I think my life has entailed a lot of struggle; sometimes I feel I set my feminist standards too high at my own personal expense. Many of us thought we could do it all – fight the establishment, hold down full-time jobs, raise our children, have significant friends and lovers, be financially independent.

I definitely suffered constantly from imposter syndrome, feeling that I was a fraud who would soon be uncovered. I just didn't come from the right class background to be an architect (my father was a second-hand car dealer in Croydon, and I'd never felt I quite fitted in to the Surrey gentility he aspiringly moved us into). I alleviated the stresses of 'doing and being it all' by drinking a lot. Luckily, I have a constitution that could cope with it, but I'm not sure my performance at work benefited. I have to say I owe an enormous amount to the people across all the (public sector) institutions I worked in who had faith in me. From the rather right-wing professor who first allowed me into the Bartlett School of Architecture without the right qualifications, to the many managers who had faith in my enthusiasm and politics and encouraged my commitment to empowering the users of the buildings I designed. Two institutions financed me to set up a design service for women, one in London and one in Sheffield.

A local authority and housing association supported us, all women, to design and build the first co-housing development in Sheffield, where I still live.

So – to go back to that turning point: what would that young woman sitting on the cold park bench think of how her decision affected the rest of her life, and how she is now in her old age? Hmm – I think she would be proud of me.

Jenny Rathbone MISS WORLD PROTESTOR AND LABOUR MP, SENEDD, WALES, CURRENTLY THE ONLY LABOUR GOVERNMENT IN THE UK

From a middle-class background, I was born in 1950 and grew up in Liverpool. We lived in a cul-de-sac in Liverpool 8 in quite a mixed community. My gang included two single parent families, one with Dad in prison, the other, son of a Black American GI. I was allowed to roam the streets quite freely until puberty started to make that more difficult. Unlike many of my primary school contemporaries, I was fully aware of the levels of poverty all around me.

Aged eleven, I was packed off to a boarding school in the south of England. I'm sure my mother thought she was doing the right thing, she'd been a pupil there in the late 1920s following the death of her father (PTSD suicide from WWI) – but what had been a progressive school in her time was by this time an ugly bastion of the status quo, preparing girls for marriage. I was bullied by other pupils and staff, very unhappy and rebelled against the ridiculous rules but never thought of running away. The prejudice abated somewhat with Beatlemania; suddenly Liverpool was a cool place to have come from.

My mother always insisted I needed a career before getting married and was encouraging me to be a social worker. I started working for a Liverpool housing association but following six months in France, I decided I wanted to go to university and get a degree. I had always wanted to be a journalist, not encouraged by the family.

My political interest was no doubt influenced by the towering legacy of my great aunt, Eleanor Rathbone, described by one historian as the most important feminist of the inter-war years; and other ancestors whose liberal non-conformist backgrounds put them in conflict with their class. Anti-slavers, municipal reformers, founder of District Nursing and so on.

My father was very close to Eleanor and she encouraged him to go to Russia with the Webbs and the Muggeridges in 1933 and to get stuck into raising medical aid for the Spanish Republicans.

My father was asked to leave the London School of Economics after one year and return to Liverpool to rescue the family business – his father was a gambler. The revelations of the Stalinist gulag in the 1950s changed his political outlook and he became a one-nation Tory. He wasn't pleased when I became Secretary of the Merseyside anarchists! All this helped shape my political moorings.

The evidence of class and sexual inequality was all around me as a child. Radicalised by my experience as a student in France in May 1968 in Grenoble, back in Liverpool I was involved in the campaign against 'In Place of Strife', Barbara Castle's proposals for limiting trade union activity. I only started getting involved in feminist politics as a student at the University of Essex in the autumn of 1969 and attended the feminist conference at Ruskin College in 1970.

Before that I had been involved in the anti-apartheid movement to stop the Springboks tour by occupying the pitch during rugby matches. I also occupied a Barclays Bank to protest at their investment in racist South Africa. Protesting at the Miss World competition was all part of my attempt to help re-shape the world to be a better place.

Was I happy? In part. I was always quite bold but underneath lacked confidence in myself. I was keen to challenge the established order of things where women were second-class citizens. I don't think I agonised about my body, but probably didn't value myself as much as I should have done. Initially I thought I didn't have a problem, that I hadn't experienced sexism. Just shows the journey we all had to travel. Betty Friedan, Germaine Greer, Susan Sontag, Jean Franco, the Cuban revolution, the 1972 miners' strike all influenced my thinking. I saw the Miss World Contest as a meat market, commercial exploitation organised by men.

I managed to get into the Albert Hall without being stopped and joined up with Jenny Fortune and others to the left of the stage. Physically fit, I managed to get at least one of my flour bombs onto the stage and remember being delighted when Bob Hope was forced to retreat off stage and the competition was suspended.

After university, I did research in Mexico on the status of women there and observed how women became more oppressed once they migrated from rural areas to the cities as they no longer had any direct control over the means of production. I experienced the flood of refugees fleeing to Mexico from Chile following the military coup against President Allende in September 1973. Returning to Britain at the end of 1974, I became a journalist, initially writing about Britain for Latin America.

I worked in current affairs television for twenty years, mainly on Granada's World in Action and the BBC Money Programme, as well as a three-part series on the international debt crisis for Channel 4. From 2002 to 2007, I managed a Sure Start programme in one of the poorest areas of north London, which included working with pregnant women and mothers with babies in Holloway Prison.

I have represented Cardiff Central in the Welsh Assembly since 2011. Wales is currently the only part of the UK with a Labour Government. I chair the Cross-Party Group on Women's Health which has achieved improved access to early medical abortion and better Period Dignity (an initiative to provide free sanitary products in schools) as well as contributing to the Well-being of Future Generations (Wales) Act 2015, a feminist document.

'Success!'
Jenny Fortune 2020

Angie Shrubsole-Brett WAS IN THE WOMEN'S STREET THEATRE SEEN IN SUE CROCKFORD'S FILM OF THE WOMEN'S MARCH 1971. THE GRASSROOTS ACTIVISM OF THE LATE 60S/70S UNDERPINNED A FULL-ON WORKING LIFE IN EDUCATION, THEATRE AND THE CREATIVE ARTS. 'THE PERSONAL IS POLITICAL' REMAINS HER MANTRA. "NOW LIVING IN SUSSEX, I'M PROUD TO SAY MY OFFSPRING CARRY ON THE TRADITION TO STRIVE FOR A FAIR SOCIETY. IT'S JUST A SHAME THE NEED TO FIGHT IS AS STRONG AS IT'S EVER BEEN...."

In 1967-70 I was studying Comparative Literature at Essex University and experiencing all the challenges of living in a highly political environment. It was impossible not to be political at Essex – although I'm sure some managed it! The place was vibrant during this period: meaningful discussions took place everywhere and at any time. The structure of the university and the schools of study, particularly Latin American and Russian departments, made it unavoidable not to want change. Revolution was in the air: sit ins, festivals, the questioning of hierarchical structures – but no feminist debate! Was I happy? Not particularly. It was very confusing. My political heart was in the right place, but all these events were led by vocal men, dominated by the male ego. Meanwhile women were trying to make sense of a world where the so-called sexual revolution was enslaving them, still satisfying the demands of men. We convinced ourselves we were liberated, but we were not. Feminism was never mentioned, and we were complicit in this through ignorance. I look back at this time and would not wish to return there, despite the political education that was going on. Essex was a special place – I do not regret going there – but it was flawed and problematic.

Generally there was a lack of female confidence: for example I have never been happy with my body. I lacked belief in my physical self and yet had no reason to feel like that. I do not think women were generally supportive or loyal to each other. Although female friends were important, as yet we had not the language to converse, to trust and therefore to be honest about our insecurities with each other. We were on the cusp of questioning the female role in life, the expectations and aspirations.

Me: I was a kind, enthusiastic and rather dramatic young woman. I was a natural socialist in many ways: desperate for a caring, equal society to be the norm, but I was not particularly articulate. And yet I was still trying to be a good daughter (of a high-ranking policeman!) whilst rejecting everything my parents had worked so hard to achieve after the poverty of the thirties and the War. How confusing it must have been for them.

I had grown up in an aspirational middle-class home in a 'good' part of London. I went to a girls' grammar school, which I now appreciate as being far more radical in its education and vision for women than I gave it credit for.

I loved the arts, and being in London I had easy access to galleries, theatres and music. These were my passions. I was averagely bright. On the surface confident, but not really. I had a restlessness and romantic thread running through me that wanted change. I had close female friends and loved the time spent with them. But boy friends were also a necessary badge of honour. The '60s was a challenging and vibrant decade to be young – and I was very much a child of that era.

During my last year at Essex, 69/70, there were the first rumblings of the emerging second wave women's movement. Awareness was beginning to change. Initially sceptical, I was, however, so ready to embrace a movement that would, amongst other things, help me understand myself and give me the strength to speak up for my beliefs.

After leaving Essex I moved back to London and started post-graduate study at Goldsmiths (Drama 1970). The Women's Liberation Workshop local groups were being formed and I joined the Battersea Group. There were roughly ten of us meeting regularly. It was an empowering and exciting time feeling you were part of a new and dynamic movement. I don't remember how we actually came together but it was a varied and fascinating group of women: I remember a very political Spanish woman and an American who was particularly good at getting out early to put 'this ad degrades women' stickers on the underground before it got too busy!

I think the small local nature of these groups was a particularly genius construct. It did not intimidate anyone and provided a supportive space for women to share and grow. Our group was keen on performance – agitprop. We took our (rather naïve!) piece on women and work to the Oxford conference. We were also part of the group caught on film by Sue Crockford dancing in the streets to 'Stay Young and Beautiful' at the Women's march in 1971.

Women's Liberation March, London, 6 March 1971: Photo © Sally Fraser.

It was such fun when I spotted myself in the clip used in The People's Century (a BBC/PBS television documentary series that examined the 20th century) – this is what your ma was doing, kids! It was certainly a movement born of optimism that we could change things.

The Miss World Demonstration in 1970 was a real wake-up call to any residue of embedded and accepted sexism. We had grown up with this wretched cattle market and accepted its premise as all-round family entertainment. Now we were seeing it for what it was – and it was gross.

I remember, and was impressed by, the bush telegraph that ensured so many women and women's groups heard about the planned demo but without the authorities getting wind of it.

It was bitterly cold and the Battersea group went together to demonstrate outside the venue. There was quite a large police presence but you felt they were not sure what was going to happen. And neither were we! I do remember, with a sheepish smile, as we were watching the smartly dressed ticket holders going past into the hall, spotting a couple of friends from Essex in their Oxfam finery. Like idiots we hugged each other, saying hello and quickly realising how foolish this was! We pulled ourselves together and became sensible! Could have blown the whole thing!

The tussles outside the hall were manipulated by groups of agitators, particularly young men, who were determined to stir things up and create a scene. They wanted those of us demonstrating to get riled up and be arrested. At one point a young PC grabbed my arm. We stared at each other. Then a sister pulled my other arm and I was free. I don't think either of us (PC and me) knew really what we were meant to do! It was a good thing I wasn't arrested that night because I had had no briefing or preparation for such an occurrence.

Meanwhile we had no real way of knowing how it was going inside.

We saw a few women sitting in police vans but we were prevented from communicating with them. The demonstration then melted away.

Only later did we fully appreciate what a remarkable event it had been. I still think the women that went inside were totally brave and amazing. I am in awe of how they confronted the establishment and the ghastly 'national treasure' that was Bob Hope. He certainly revealed his true colours. I'm glad he was scared.

I'm proud to have played a small part in this creative, colourful, political demonstration. It was a genius idea and incredibly well planned. I believe the whole episode played a significant part in the history of the Women's Liberation Movement – and for that we can be rightly proud.

Facing and following pages >>
Reproduction of pamphlet produced in 1971 to answer the question 'Why Miss World?'

WHY MISS WORLD?
WHY WHY WORLD
MISS WHY?
WHY ORLD
WHY MIS MISS
WORLD WHY?
MISS WORLD
WHY? WHY?
MISS WO HY MISS
WORLD MISS WORLD
WHY MISS ORLD WHY MISS
ORLD? Y MISS WORLD
WHY? ISS WORLD WHY
WHY MISS WORLD WHY?
WHY WHY MISS WORLD?

THE COMPETITION WILL SOON BE OVER

.....WE HAVE BEEN IN THE MISS WORLD **CONTEST** ALL OUR LIVES......

JUDGING OURSELVES AS THE JUDGES JUDGE US - LIVING TO PLEASE **MEN** -

DIVIDING OTHER W**O**MEN UP INTO SAFE FRIENDS AND ATTRACTIVE RIVALS -

GRADED, DEGRADED, HUMILIATED...........WE'VE SEEN THROUGH IT.

MECCA ARE SUPERPIMPS SELLING WOMEN'S BODIES TO FRUSTRATED VOYEURS UNTIL

AGEING BUSINESSMEN JUMP **YOUNG** GIRLS IN DARK ALLEYS - BUT THEY'RE ONLY

SMALL-TIME PIMPS IN OUR EVERYDAY PROSTITUTION: WOMEN'S BODIES USED BY

BUSINESSMEN TO SELL THEIR GARBAGE - LEGS SELLING STOCKINGS, CORSETS

SELLING WAISTS, CUNTS SELLING DEODARANTS, MARY QUANT SELLING SEX......OUR

SEXUALITY HAS BEEN TAKEN AWAY FROM US, TURNED INTO MONEY FOR SOMEONE ELSE,

THEN RETURNED DEADENED BY ANXIETY.

WOMEN WATCHING...............................WHY ARE YOU HERE?

THE MAN'S MAKING MONEY OUT OF US — WE'RE NOT BEAUTIFUL OR UGLY WE'RE ANGRY

THE MANS MAKING

The first Miss World contest took place in 1951. It coincided with the festival of Britain, a centenary of the Great Exhibition, which celebrated the Nation's brave post-war recovery and demonstrated its continued technological inventiveness. Techonological innovations are essential to capitalism. They stimulate production and thereby in crease profits:- provided that new markets are secured both at home and abroad.

At the Festival Hall on the South Bank leading manufacturers displayed up-to-date items of interest for international consumption, with the firm intention of putting Britain once more 'on the map'. On the North Bank, at the Lyceum, Mecca Ltd presented their new invention – an international beauty contest. The organiser, Eric Morley, lamented the fact that, 'in those days some countries hadn't even heard of beauty contests'. So of course, he congratulates the company bosses for 'shrewdly anticipating the public appetite for such an event'. The 'event' has made Mecca into a £20 million enterprise.

In the Miss World Story Morley tells how he 'made it', and, like most tales of entrepreneurial heroism, it's a matter of transforming petty thieving into respectable big business. Prior to the Miss World contest, Mecca ball- rooms throughout the country had been running contests of the 'outright'- that is, outdated – type. Local girls paraded in bikinis, or stars and G-strings and were disqualified by the audience jeering at their 'under-or over-weight statistics'. (These contests were probably derivative of carnival culture, and as such at least had more vitality than the slick hence more insidious prefabrication of Miss World.)

The new brand of contestants, unlike those of the 'outright' type, were seen as National Representatives selected in order to stand up to international competition. To start with Morley looks for what he calls 'basic material': girls between 17 and 25, ideally 5ft 7½", 8 or 9 stone, waist 22-24", hips 35- 36", bust 36-37", "no more no less", a lovely face, good teeth, plenty of hair and perfectly shaped legs from front and back – carefully checked for 'such defects as slightly knocked knees'. Then with the basic material' plus the aid of cosmetics and a deportment school, he manufactures the 'perfect product'. It is a sound capital investment since overheads are low. First of all, raw material is practically free. Morely proudly affirms that he refuses to pay the girls travelling expenses, gives them only board and lodging and a small allowance. Secondly, labour, represented by performance, is unpaid except for the winners £2,500. Mecca makes up for this in the long run since Miss World is obliged to sign a contract for future appearances. The contestants were forced to make so many appearances that as early as 1952 they threatened to go on strike. Obviuosly this wasn't in the 'public interest' and the girls weren't even accorded the sparse dignity of union-style negotiations. Morley, giving himself a man-sized pat in the back for his expertise in 'human relations' settled, or rather pre-empted, the dispute by rushing out and buying each girl a teddy bear '.

MONEY OUT OF US

'Human relations' under capitalism means the art of exacting services from a subordinate without provoking a consequent sense of injustice. Applied to women, 'human relations' means exaggerated paternalism or diluted chivalry. The first approach insists that women are like children and therefore respond to scolding or pampering. As Morley said of the dissident contestants' reactions to his teddy bear ploy 'they are all sweetness and smiles again'. The other approach senses the injustice of womens inferior social position but suggests that polite gestures are sufficient compensation. The Miss World contestants caricature the alienating effects of selling ones labour —they are literally engaged in selling 'themselves'.

Married women are banned from the contest because, Morley explains, 'It might make a woman dissatisfied with her life as housewife and mother . . . husbands ought to have their brains tested if they allow it'. As for the contestants 'reputation', this is ensured by chaperones who 'rule the girls like Holloway prison warders'. Respectability ultimately has a class connotation, he continues 'this contest is no longer degrading, because unlike the fifties when it was the sort of thing girls of the so-called lower classes did . . . now we have daughters of some titled people, a number from wealthy families or of public school education'.

There is no question of 'fixing'the contests, but to get the 'right' girls, you have to get the 'right' judges. They mustlook for more than a 'busty girl with a sweet face'. Competition is no longer with the girl round the corner, but with the girls in the sunsilk ad. Mecca make a substantial sum by selling the rights to televise the contest. This means that the entrant better be able to read a script, speak into a mike without stuttering, and generally look good on TV.

Over 27 million people watch the Miss World specatacle. They see racism carefully concealed behind the 'family of nations'facade; Miss Grenada can become Miss World, make obliging remarks about the British hospitality, and consequently pacify 2 million under-paid immigrant workers. A miss White south Africa and a Miss Black South Africa make it possible to pretend, at least for an evening, that apartheid is not so definitive. Miss India, during her reign as Miss World, entertained American troops in Vietnam, and'received cheers in spite of being coloured and wearing a saree'(Bob Hope) The Miss Third World trend reflected the 'wind of change'-a view of the world as a happy family of united nations engaged in peaceful competition rather than violent confrontation. This ideology served to obscure the anti-imperialist struggles at home and abroad. In fact, post-war retention of foreign markets has meant that Britain has had to intervene in, or at least condone the repression of national liberation fronts in places like the West Indies, South Africa, India and the Arab Gulf – even today RAF planes are bombing the small villages of Dhofar held by the NLF.   (contd)

MECCA

MANAGING-DIRECTOR - Eric Morley

BINGO · DANCING CASINOS · GOLDEN Q CLUBS · CATERING L.VOUCHS · PROMOTIONS

AGENCY BANDS CABARET · SCOTIA AMUSEMENTS · WORLD DANCING CHAMPS · SILVER BLADES · HAMMERSMITH PALAIS

DEAL FRENCHY · DIRECT MAIL · INSURANCE AGENTS · WHOLE SALE PAPER · PRINTING + TRAVEL

TAKEOVER in 1970 – £33m!

4

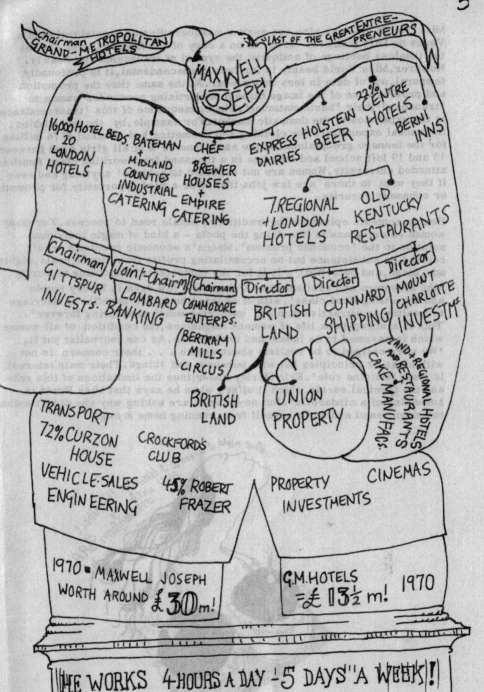

Chairman METROPOLITAN GRAND HOTELS

LAST OF THE GREAT ENTREPRENEURS

MAXWELL JOSEPH

16,000 HOTEL BEDS. BATEMAN 20 LONDON HOTELS

MIDLAND COUNTIES INDUSTRIAL CATERING

CHEF + BREWER HOUSES + EMPIRE CATERING

EXPRESS DAIRIES

HOLSTEIN BEER

22% CENTRE HOTELS

BERNI INNS

7. REGIONAL + LONDON HOTELS

OLD KENTUCKY RESTAURANTS

Chairman GITTSPUR INVESTS.

Joint-Chairm. LOMBARD BANKING

Chairman COMMODORE ENTERPS.

Director BRITISH LAND

Director CUNNARD SHIPPING

Director MOUNT CHARLOTTE INVESTM.

(BERTRAM MILLS CIRCUS)

LAND + REGIONAL HOTELS AND RESTAURANTS CAKE MANUFACS.

BRITISH LAND

UNION PROPERTY

TRANSPORT 72% CURZON HOUSE

CROCKFORD'S CLUB

BRITISH LAND

VEHICLE-SALES ENGINEERING

45% ROBERT FRAZER

PROPERTY INVESTMENTS

CINEMAS

1970 = MAXWELL JOSEPH WORTH AROUND £30m!

G.M.HOTELS = £13½ m! 1970

HE WORKS 4 HOURS A DAY – 5 DAYS "A WEEK"!

Miss World viewers also see sexism masquerading as a celebration of a Venus de Milo (cameras zoom in on a copy of the famous Greek statue) the timeless heritage of antiquity, the symbol of transcendental beauty. Howerer, Miss World beauty is far from transcendental, it is profoundly temporal, out of date in less than a year. At the same time the promotion and proliferation of the image through advertising persuades women to 'transcend' their 'basic material'. The consequence of this 'transcendance' is the expansion of the domestic market. For example, by the mid-sixties, the annual expenditure for clothing and cosmetics had reached £174 million for the teenage group alone. At the same time 70 % of all girls aged between 15 and 19 left school and only one in a thousand from working class families attended university. Women are not expected to 'achieve' anything and even if they want to there are few jobs that offer a real opportunity for promotion or economic security.

Beauty contests epitomise the traditional female road to success. For many women entering one is like doing the pools – a kind of magic individual solution to the 'economic problem'. Mecca's economic problems aren't centred on subsistence but on accumulating profits from finals, heats, rights, ads, bingo, and bets. What's in it for the contestants? According to Morley, 'the adventure and excitement of living for a few days in luxury hotels and travelling first class', with of course 'the fringe benefits of marriage to wealthy or attractive men and memories worth treasuring forever'. This is a scrap-book life of womens magazines, the condition of all women which is assumed to be innate and unalterable. As one journalist put it, 'We were obliged to be realists about women . . . their concern is not with ideas or principles but with persons and things. Their main interest is their feminine role'. Eric Morley underlines the limitations of this role and the farcical escape which it offers when he says that Miss World is something of a cindarella'. But now women are asking why she didn't seize the magic wand and save herself from running home in rags.

Last night I dreamt I blew up the Albert Hall with my Maidenform BRA...

Twelve years old – I was beginning to become aware of myself as
a woman – and of how my friends were becoming women. The
badges and proof of womanhood were bras, makeup, stockings and
boyfriends, and it was up to each one of us to adopt these badges
as quickly and successfully as possible. I didn't like the idea at
all at first, I hated the thought of having to change so radically,
just in order to prove my womanhood. But gradually, more and
more of my friends were wearing bras, having periods, going out
with boys. Gradually I stopped resisting their ideas of womanhood
– I didn't want to seem different, be a freak. I started scanning
the fashion magazines as avidly as my friends, started going to
parties to flirt, grope and neck with guys, all the while slightly
horrified at what I was doing to myself, feeling myself slowly
becoming buried under layers and layers of 'femininity', finding
myself becoming more and more passive.

The whole of my life seems the same – time after time, being afraid
to be different or assert myself, my individuality and identity. I
wanted to be the kind of woman that the ads. magazines, telly, etc.
told me to be – tender charming, gay, attractive – men complimented
me on being a good listener, 'sympathetic', 'tolerant', it made me
feel warm inside to know that I was so good at being a woman.

At university, I heard about Women's Liberation and didn't like
what I heard. It sounded as though W.L. was about women asser-
ting themselves, having their own opinions, making their own decisions, independently of men. Horrible! I thought, impossible,
frightening.

The thought seemed to open up a big gaping hole which I was going
to lose myself down if I didn't forget about those ideas immediately.
But there remained a little question mark in my mind that became
more and more impossible to ignore. It twisted and wriggled, gla-
red like a neon sign and finally exploded .....

I WAS ANGRY.

I COULD BE ANGRY.

I'd been conned
swindled out of knowing myself.

I'd believed that
I was what the adman
told me I was.
And oh, the relief
of knowing that I
wasn't, didn't have to behave in the right ways any longer to prove
that I was a success at being a woman. It opened up boundless pos-
sibilities. I started discovering that I liked women and started to
trust some

MISS WORLD

This account was put together by several people who took part in the Miss World demonstration. It gives only a partial view of what happened and does not include the views of everyone involved.

The Miss World Competition is not an erotic exhibition; it is a public celebration of the traditional female road to success. The Albert Hall on the evening of November 20th. was miles away from the underground world of pornography. The atmosphere was emphatically respectable, enlivened by contrived attempts at 'glamour'. The conventionality of the girls' lives and the ordinariness of their aspirations, -Miss Grenada(Miss World);

"Now I'm looking for the ideal man to marry"

- was the keynote of all the pre-and post- competition publicity. Their condition is the condition of all women, born to be defined by their physical attributes, born to give birth, or if born pretty, born lucky, a condition which makes it possible and acceptable within the bourgeois ethic, for girls to parade, silent and smiling, to be judged on the merits of their figures and faces. (Bob Hope- "Pretty girls don't have those problems." ie, the problems that plain girls have in finding a husband or making a successful career. W.L.girls must be plain, because only plain girls would have an interest in attacking the system.)Demonstrating against Miss World, Women's Liberation struck a blow against this narrow destiny, against the physical confines of the way women are seen and the way they fit into society. Most of all it was a blow against passivity, not only the enforced passivity of the girls on the stage, but the passivity that we all felt in ourselves, We were dominated while preparing for the demonstration by terror at what we were about to do. - To take violent action, interrupting a carefully ordered spectacle, drawing attention to ourselves, inviting the hostility of thousands of people was something that we had all previously thought to be personally impossible for us, inhibited both by our conditioning as women, and our acceptance of bourgeois norms of correct behaviour. It was a revolt against the safeness of our lives, the comfort of continual contact with like-minded people. The fact of joining W.L. shows a level of awareness of women's condition. But it's also possible within the movement to become sheltered by the support and understanding of a group, and/or friends. In the Albert Hall we were back in the previous isolation of the outside world, surrounded by people, men and women who were there to participate in the oppression of women. And who were outraged and bewildered by our challenge to it. The outside world is mystified, and consequently often hostile, but W.L. cannot for that reason fear communication with it. Women must be confident enough to challenge the distortion or indifference of the Press and transcend their own feelings of vulnerability.

The seating arrangements in the Albert Hall were completely different from what we had expected. For example, Sally and I found ourselves unexpectedly isolated on the other side of the hall from most of the others ; we had only managed to fill the two extra seats at the last moment; Laura found herself downstairs, instead of upstairs. We had reduced our grandiose plans to the simplest strategy of aiming for the jury and the stage with the comic array of weapons with which we were armed. We got into the hall amazingly easily, we thought, what with the Young Liberals' propaganda, the bomb scare, and strict security, that a group of unescorted girls would never be allowed in. Once seated, Sally and I realised that the hall itself wasn't nearly as vast as our heightened imaginations had led us to believe. Above all we saw how ludicrously accessible the stage was, and that our only possible plan could be to make for the stage. Our feelings ranged from complicity with the audience - a mixture of people backing their own national candidates, to overdressed couples on a night out and the odd family outing - mixed with an intense feeling that we stood out, and that everyone was staring at us. The conspiratorial non-acknowledgement of each other in the ladies' and the intermission - silent solidarity. Mostly it was the feeling of being caged in, surrounded by superficially 'nice' but basically hostile thousands.

In the hall, Sally's and my conversation fluctuated wildly between frantically whispered consultations of mutual encouragement, and overloud comments about the show, the judges, the girls, anything 'ordinary', and unsuspicious. We tried our best to laugh at Bob Hope's jokes, in a pathetic attempt to feel one with the audience at last. But as joke after joke fell flat, we were even isolated in our affort at normality. Suddenly the signal which we had been waiting for so anxiously, came at the perfect moment. It was our robot-like response which surprised us most of all. When the moment came, it was easier to act than to consider; in the scuffle with the police, it was anger and determination that prevailed. As I was lifted bodily out of the hall, three Miss Worlds came running up to me, a trio of

sequined, perfumed visions, saying; "Are you alright?""Let her go" When the policeman explained we were from W.L. and demonstrating against them, I managed to say that we weren't against them we were FOR them, but against Mecca and their exploitation of women. "Come on Miss Venezuala, we're on" and the trio disappeared down the corridor. Then I was dragged off, and taken to a room where to my relief, I saw that Sally and the two girls who gave the signal had already been detained.

How was it, with so many odds against us, that the demonstration was successful?

The spectacle is vulnerable. However intricately planned it is, a handful of people can disrupt it and cause chaos in a seemingly impenetrable organisation. The spectacle isn't prepared for anything other than passive spectators.

Bob Hope made more connections than we ever hoped to put across; his continual emphasis on Vietnam revealed the arrogance of imperialism behind the supposedly reassuring family of nations facade.

The Press, searching for sensations, turned a small demonstration into headline news. Let's leave the last words to Bob Hope; "They said we were 'using' women. I always thought we were using them right. I don't want to change position with them. Why do they want to change position with me?

I don't want to have babies, I'M TOO BUSY."

Women met from
groups around
London who had
been thinking
and talking about
women's liber-
ation for quite a
while. There
were differences
and antagonism,
a lot of tension
— the only thing
we were all
agreed on was
wanting to stop
the contest

This is the
spectacle mill-
ions of people
were watching
— the ponces,
the pimps,
the role —
players, acting
out the sordid
spectacle
between them.

Bob Hope was too much to be able
to take — spontaneously, two
women gave the pre-arranged
signal — a whistle —
and the hall erupted.

MISS WORLD IS A MAN'S WORLD

THE SPECTACLE SHATTERS AS

We threw smoke bombs, flour, stink bombs, leaflets, blew whistles, waved rattles – Bob Hope freaked out, ran off the stage. We got thrown out by Mecca bouncers: Sally was arrested for assault (stubbing her cigarette out on a police-pig). Jenny was done for an offensive weapon (a children's smoke bomb). Some went on to the Cafe de Paris where the Miss Worlds were having dinner – two more arrests – Jo and Kate for throwing flour and rotten tomatoes at the Mecca pimps. Maia was arrested for abusive language (telling a pig to fuck off) – her charge was dismissed early on in the case.

AFTER THE BAIL WAS OVER.

After that, for a few of us, came the decision as to whether we were going to defend ourselves in court and explain in that way why we had demonstrated and what we were fighting. I was coming face to face with the law and it looked like this ...

I was scared – scared to assert myself in the face of the law of the land. Why shouldn't I try and get off with a light sentence? Admit I was guilty. A lawyer could defend me better than myself.

WE EACH REACTED DIFFERENTLY TO THINKING OF THE TRIAL

Small charges – first offences. Easy way out – play it straight, get a lawyer (employ an expert to represent me and say It better (what, Why?) implying – get it over with ...) Plead GUILTY ... Why?

Because that's a whole contradiction to a whole action which was Joyful ... So what's the point of adopting a new clean-clothed, safe, tamed, timid, intimidating Woman Image, if it means standing in a public dock box and mouthing the words ... "I am guilty... of insulting behaviour". It's not true, and saying we caused a breach of the Peace (insulting whom and whose peace are we breaching?).

DEFEND. WHAT ? What are we defending ?

QUESTIONS,in my nerves are lit, Yet you know there is no answer
yet. Questions, Questions, are forming all the time...What are we defending? We will be on trial. What for? Individual acts or Womens Liberation?

DEFEND

All our lives we had been letting other people defend us, speak for
us, lead us, apologise for us. This was a chance to change that,
TO SPEAK FOR OURSELVES, break through our passivity, and
that led to challenging too the role that lawyers played, in society,

Experts, well-oiled in legal jargon, ready to defend any persons acts
against the system, but never to step over that line and challenge the
basis of the Law.This was confirmed by various lawyers re-actions-
like,a Woman Barrister saying "I can defend Women's Liberation , but
not YOUR actions."
And "Be prepared for a psychiatric report."
And another "Just think of me as a mechanic with a garage of
legal information" - OUT of the garage and INTO the Streets
we chorused to him.
And Womens' Liberation Workshop said that this is the first
trial since the suffragettes. You'll not be articulate or
confident - you'll be smashed - and We don't want martyrs.

SO WE BEGAN TO THINK WHAT DO WE WANT OUT OF THE
TRIAL. AND WHO ARE WE?

AND by thinking of ways of challenging we begin to feel confidence from working together, knowing that we can emerge from
Conditioned Responses, remembering the joy and strength of
that togetherness feeling in the Albert Hall, jumping from the
seats, racing down the aisles, shattering the Spectacle of BEAUTY
and saying What the fuck is this all about. What is happening to Women?

AND realising how a scream can be a public event - meaning
let's make public, let it out, the stifling feelings, keep no more,
making secret safe silent shameful ... private, let's change,
challenge, bring into the open, expose, abolish ... the Private,
privates, Property. Screams, War-cries ... becoming weapons
that mean transforming the guilt-defences - passivity - soft -
inexpressed - sacrificial thoughts that are STATIC.

AND remembering in the court room the first time we came up
(to be remanded on bail) the emphasis on being and keeping
silence ... THE PEACE ... acceptance, restraint, order, suppress, pain, tears, pills, tranquilizers, sleep, peace, calm,
soft PASSIVITY ... KEEP calm, accept society, and SILENCE
IN COURT ... the lawyer will speak, the magistrate will answer
... the Soft Process continues ... knowing that the "common

prostitutes" we spent the night with in the cells when we were
remanded, will follow us in and plead 'guilty' -because it's
easier - the policeman said so, so why bother to question what
'guilty' or words, or 'justice' means ... 'just get it over with
quick love'.

AND remembering and realising   ... I wanted to scream, make
some sound, some Human NOISE to shatter the silent static pro-
cedure, the soft mysterious process that envelops ...
    "werenotgonnatakeit ... We're not gonna TAKE it".

Suddenly the roaring horror of my own passivity hit me in the face.
The years and years of lack of faith in myself were all rearing
their ugly faces and jeering at me - you, defend yourself'. they
said - you must be joking! Who do you think is going to take someone like you seriously. You'll be smashed and spat upon, you
won't even be able to open your mouth to say a thing in court,
you'll be so scared.
That's right, I thought, that's myself speaking after all. But
the only trouble was that that was the part of myself I didn't
like at all. It was the part of myself that was always making
excuses for myself, always backing out of things, hiding behind
an image of helplessness and lack of confidence. I didn't want
to be like that. I wanted to escape from all that, throw it away,
and I knew that the only way I was going to do that was by defying
it and saying 'no, I'm not like that. I can stand up in that court
and speak for myself along with the other women, and fighting
the weakenss I feel by myself'.

                 These were our thoughts, fears, hopes,
                 that we went through before the trial.
                 And it was getting clearer that:

We wanted to go further than defending ourselves.
We wanted to ATTACK;
- the law that had arrested us, the court that was sentencing
us, and show how it was part of a system based on the protection
of private property interests.
We wanted to
- break down the structure of the court itself and the Isolation
of being on a trial as an Individual, feeling intimidated by the
Court, the Law, the Science, the Mystery.

THAT MEANT ... challenging the court at every point.
- by speaking to each other in our own language that would be
understandable to anyone.
- by speaking to our witnesses ourselves, as they were the
women we demonstrated with,
- and explaining that way why we wanted to stop the contest.
- by using the court to talk to other women and to CREATE
a space in the court. HOW?

WHAT HAPPENED IN COURT. . . . .

WE STARTED THE TRIAL.

1. By trying to make the actual courtroom less formal – by demanding the right to have friends as legal advisors (for the three of us without lawyers). We found a previous case (Mc-Kenzie v. McKenzie) gave a precedent for this; which meant sitting with friends, instead of sitting alone in the dock.

2. We requested for our 4 cases to be heard together.

3. We started by pleading "not guilty" – "we've been guilty all our lives as women and we won't plead guilty any more".

4. We challenged the Bench and the Magistrate – explaining that as they had a "vested and pecuniary interest in the verdict" (ie paid male) they had no right to judge us. For a man shall not be judge in his own cause.

So we did it, and the reality was a tremendous feeling of exhilaration and joy. We were fighting back on our own terms, refusing too be humbled by the court, laughing in it's face, feeling tremendous confidence and trust in each other.
They spun it out over 5 days, with as much as a month and a half in between, but in spite of that, the confidence of the women on trial built up and up until the court was being held on our terms- we were beginning to say what we wanted to and learning and showing what justice is – a farce.
The Magistrate was patronising and stifling. He became Daddy, dispensing wisdom to his naughty but intelligent daughters. So we ignore him effectively. by continuing to talk to each other and our witnesses about our lives..."What do you think of the magistrate?" we ask, "He is irrelevant". Finally his patience gets thin..BECAUSE..

DADDY IS NOT FAIR OR HONEST ... HE IS ANGRY.

The Sick comedy turns really sour as the power is turned on. Witnesses were dragged out of the witness box. On the last day but one three women (all of them witnesses) were illegally detained outside the courtroom by Special Branch and CID filth.

But the show goes on ... Justice must be SEEN to be DONE.

When Jo (six months pregnant) tried to leave the courtroom to get a lawyer for the three women, she was thrown to the ground by six pigs. In the fight that followed one woman was arrested for assault, and the three were dragged off without being arrested or charged, and held in Barnet police station for 9 hours before they were released. They were interrogated about the bombing at the house of Robert Carr on January 12th, the bombing of the BBC van the night before the Miss World Contest, their politics, their friends, their kids ("who does he belong to anyway?), their sexuality ("you're butch aren't you?).

The four defendants spent that night in Holloway, and were interrogated about the bombing the next day before they appeared in

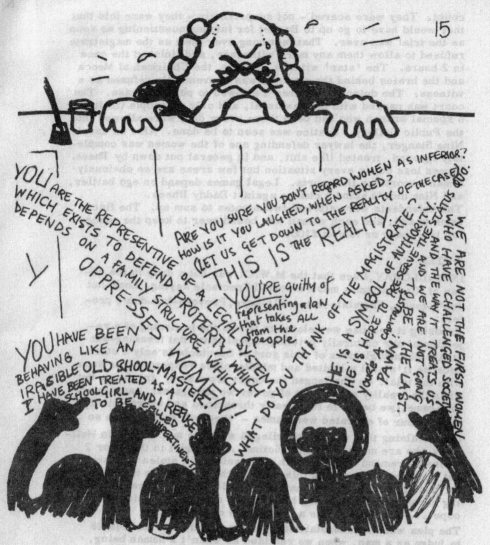

I felt that the event symbolised my daily exploitation. I saw the contestants
being judged my men, and I know what it feels like to be judged and scrutinised every day when I am just walking down the street. I saw women
being forced to compete with each other and being judged by men. I felt for
them. I had no intention of hurting them or attacking them in any way.
We did not throw anything on to the stage when the contestants were
there. We threw missiles on the stage when Bob Hope was speaking.
In the same way we threw nothing when the Miss World contestants were
going into the Cafe de Paris. This was a conscious decision. We regard
these contestants as unfortunate victims of the male capitalist system.
This system, that makes money by persuading women to buy goods such
as false eyelashes. We are sick of all this line about beauty. We are not
beautiful and we are not ugly. It is a big capitalist con."

court. They were scared – not surprisingly – they were told that they would have to go up to Barnet for further questioning as soon as the trial was over. That fact hung over them as the magistrate refused to allow them any more witnesses, and finished the case in 2 hours. The 'star' witness, Morley, the Chairman of Mecca and the brains behind the contest, was conveniently refused as a witness. The defendants weren't allowed to put their case. The court was packed with pigs as usual, and only 15 people (including 6 special branch who had been there every day) were allowed into the Public Gallery. Justice was seen to be done. Also as usual, Nina Stanger, the lawyer defending one of the women was completely ignored, treated like shit, and in general put down by Rhees. Women lose out in every situation but few areas are so obviously a man's world as the courts. Legal games depend on ego battles, and Nina didn't stand a chance against Daddy Rhees. The defendents were allowed two minutes to sum up. The fines came to £80, and each woman was bound over to keep the peace for two years or forfeit £100.

AFTER

IN HOLLOWAY, I see that the M.W.C. was but a drop in the ocean of Capitalism's mess-a sordid Spectacle saying, Look-but don't-touch, Stimulate-but-can't-have, Provoke-but-don't protest.
Exposing it because we related to it was the beginning of a rejection of our culturally privileged positions. But freaking-out at the phoney glamour of this sort of Spectacle is only a start, because it's still a limited and middle-class response. The same with the trial. We challenged the court process by freaking, but when the reality of the sort of power we areagainst, came out of that game, we began to feel really threatened and unprotectedby our armour of educated wordgames – they will only stretch so far. Realsing that we are privileged when we met women in Holloway who are much more the Victims....one girl in there for 2 weeks on remand for being in possession of a stolen license.... but then there's a woman this week in the papers, on homicide, for pushing a dummy down her own child's throat, because a whining husband was demanding his supper, and she not being able to cope....Miss World, was a drop in the ocean.......
The plea was an understatement, saying daddy was inadequate to judge as a man, when we realised he wasn't a human being, he was/is merely a TOOL. As Daddy he was comparatively harmless. A Wet liberal merely being Masculine and pompous. But he revealed himself often as the capitalist pawn and finally exposed himself as a TOOL of a powerful oppressive capitalist and imperialist Way of Life, whose liberal laws as applied mean separation and repression ... DEATH AND DIVISION ... AND ARE ...

IRRELEVANT TO LIFE
BECAUSE we know and have felt the strength that the
JOY OF THE STRUGGLE IS IN THE CREATING.
OUT OF THE COURT – INTO THE STREETS

GAY LIBERATION FRONT STREET THEATRE OUTSIDE THE COURT

"BEAUTY AND THE BOVVER GIRLS"

The MW demonstration was conceived as a propaganda action.
We calculated that groups of girls emerging from the gloom of the
auditorium waving football rattles, hurling 'weapons', shouting
slogans, and being dragged out would create enough of a counter-
spectacle to disrupt the show. As predicted, the media encouraged
by Bob Hope's hysterical reaction, moved in – the screens of 7
million viewers erupted with streamers, leaflets and chaos for
several minutes and the following day we were splashed all over
the front pages of the popular press. We had indeed drawn attention to ourselves, but we had disastrously under-estimated the
ability of the press to 'interpret' events. The pre-contest
planning meetings had unanimously rejected the use of any slogan
or action that could possibly be construed as an attack on the contestants, or that might lead us to any violent confrontation. So
we were naive enough to assume that although reaction might be
hostile, the important issues would clearly emerge and other women
would understand what we were doing. This was a miscalculation.

It was Bob Hope's impression of us as ugly bomb-throwing drug-addicts that received generous coverage. Our purpose in demonstrating and the politics of the WL movement were entirely ignored. Instead the focus was placed on our freakish personalities, our connections with left-wing extremisim, etc. etc. We had made, it seemed yet another contribution to the bra-burning, man-hating horror image of WL.

As the trial escalated into police harrassment of witnesses, suppression of the defence and intimidation of the defendents, publicity continued, undirected by us, and developed into a smear campaign. "We're not beautiful, we're not ugly, we're angry," read one of our leaflets. The Special Branch led by Det. Chief Sup. Habershon apparently under heavy pressure from the government, jumped to the conclusion that there must be some connection between the WL and the Angry Brigade. This (desperate) speculation on the part of the Special Branch had the full support of the capitalist press: "FORD BOMB: WOMEN'S LIB QUIZ BY POLICE" (Evening News 20.3.71), "ANGRY BRIGADE WOOS WOMEN MILITANTS" (Evening Standard)

The reality was rather more prosaic. We were neither vengeful harridans embittered by the sight of a pretty face, nor a tightly-knit terrorist unit. Few of us had any previous political experience most of us met for the first time over the demonstration. Some came from different WL groups up and down the country, others were on their own. We did anticipate the possibility of some police intervention. What we did not anticipate was the scale of confrontation with the forces of the state that the Miss World action unleashed. Events overtook us, and we found ourselves in a situation where it was difficult if not impossible to resist media manipulation and distortion.

The fact that about 100 girls demonstrated was almost immediately forgotten by the press. Interest focused - at least until the link-up with the Angry Brigade - exclusively on the 5 defendents. Our immediate reaction was alarm; we felt isolated, over-exposed, and even faintly ridiculous. Once the first shock of arrest etc. had died down, all our time and energy was spent on the trial. If a journalist approached us, they were rapidly passed on to someone else. As a result only the most persistent were given interviews and WL lost a crucial apportunity for communication.

This lack of positive strategy towards the media revealed the confusion and ambiguity that surrounded the Miss World action. There was an irresolvable contradition in its conception. On the one hand because the contest was an Ideological target, the intention of the demonstration was propaganda by deed, i.e. we were not deliberately recruiting, but we were attempting to make our politics and ideas accessible to other women. On the other hand we were firmly against any co-operation with the bourgeois media. There is something self-defeating in the politics of a movement which is prepared to burst onto the screens of 7 million viewers one minute, but withdraw the next into a jealously guarded privacy. To ordinary women this implies that WL is an exclusive and secret sect – something esoteric, nothing to do with their lives – when in fact our slogan exhorts all women to unite. Of course it would be foolish not to be sceptical of the capitalist media. Its function is to reproduce the ideological mystification which capitalism needs. Sexist ideology is a major component of this mystification. The media therefore must combat WL, which, by challenging sexism threatens the precarious ideological stability on which capitalism is based. Nevertheless at this stage in the struggle we are still far from having our own channels of mass communication; the left-wing press has only a small circulation, and anyway is generally suspicious of radical feminism; and the underground press is at best confused, at worst blatantly sexist. Most women therefore will only hear of our existence through telly interviews and articles in the popular press. In this context, it is important to realise that because women's liberation is newsworthy it will be discussed with or without our participation. Whether an action such as Miss World is a priority for the WL movement, may still be questioned, what is certain however, is that such action is useless as means of propaganda unless it is supported by a campaign which explains the issues involved. Propaganda by deed is not enough.

WHY MISS WORLD?

The Miss World action and the trial which followed was the first militant confrontation with the law by women since the suffragettes. It is over 60 years since Annie Kenney and Christabel Pankhurst received 3 and 7 days in Strangeways for addressing the crowd outside a meeting of the liberal candidate Winston Churchill, in Manchester. Previously they had been roughly thrown out of the hall for causing a disturbance when they asked the platform for a statement of its position on the question of votes for women. This first illegal action of the suffragettes was followed 3 years later in 1908 by the celebrated trial of Mrs Pankhurst, her daughter Christabel, and Mrs Flora Drummond. They appeared at Bow Street charged with conduct likely to cause a breach of the peace and received 2 and 3 month sentences. The witnesses included Lloyd George and Herbert Gladstone, whom they had subpoened. The Pankhursts conducted their own defence. Their cross-examination of witnesses, the speeches they made in court amounted to a brilliant exposure of male prejudice and the legal system. In the course of the trial we re-discovered the political importance of self-defence, both as a means of defending our self-respect and as a means of conscioulsy rejecting the image of female acquiescence. Self-defence is a public demonstration of our refusal to collude in our own repression. It is an expression of the politics of women's liberation.

The suffragettes didn't have to be taken seriously until their demand for the vote was linked with the unemployed agitation 1908/9, the syndicalist inspired industrial militancy in the years 1910-13, the uprise of Irish nationalism.

Now the women's liberation movement is part of the growing revolutionary movement in England, as the state shows increasing willingness to show force in varying degrees: against the catholic minority in Northern Irealnd, militant sectors of the working class, the black community, militant homosexuals and the remnants of the student movement. Radical feminism is opening out the increasing revolutionary struggle into new areas - we want control not only over the means of production but over the means of reproduction as well - which is why we are organising around abortion, contraception and childcare, questioning our sexual conditioning, changing the family structure, fighting institutions, publications and programme·s that maintain women's oppression and promote the traditional submissive female.

We are invading the public world with the private one - bringing our isolation and repression out into the open - showing they have root in the political structure, not in our individual inability to cope.

AFTER MISS WORLD

All the excitement, the release of action, joy in our strength, ended with the first remand. Everyone went home for Christmes.

We fell deeper than ever into nightmare isolation - there was no womens movement, nothing to do, just the terror of waking up in the morning with nothing to look forward to.....

The Miss World action was a reaction against humiliation, powerlessness. It wasn't part of a plan - we hadn't worked out clearly where our oppresion comes from, how the system runs on it, why we are used, how we can change it. So there was nothing to fall back on. As far as we could see the demonstration had had no effect. (In fact, the womens workshop membership doubled in the month after and a year later women were still talking about it as something that started them thinking about their oppression.)

For us, out of that vacuum, despair, we began to build ways of acting together which will make a movement over years istead of flash and disappear. We've worked more in the communities we

live in - fighting for nurseries, playhouses for our kids, working
with unsupported mothers in Claimants' Unions, meeting in small
groups. Some of us have tried to live in collectives, some have
worked with GLF. Most of it has been slow, painstaking organising
compared with the Miss World demonstration - but it's in the home
around kids, sexuality that our oppression bites deepest, holds
hardest. The 'left' have always said the economy - our exploitation has to be changed <u>first</u> before our lives, our oppression.
We say both have to be changed at once - the struggle against
internalised oppression, against how we live our lives, is where
we begin, is where we've been put. But we can't end there - it's
through that initial struggle that we understand that we cant live as
we wantto until the power structures of society have been broken.

Some of us felt that the biggest need in the womens movement was
for us to work out more clearly in what direction we are going,
what kind of change we want, so that we didn't go from demo
to demo with nothing in between. So that we had a way of
criticising what we were doing, knowing what others were doing,
understanding what we had done. The Womens Newspaper was an
attempt to do that - it was shortlived. Pamphlets like this one
could be another way.....

The Miss World action was criticized afterwards for being the
kind of action that could only be done by very confident women, a
confidence that comes from being middle-class. Most of the
demonstraters were middle-class - most of the womens movement
is - and in some ways that's a criticism. Womens oppression
cuts across class, but our roles serve capitalism, and are caused
and dictated by it. We're needed as wives and mothers to breed
and feed the producers, serve and clothe the work force; as
sexual objects to relieve our providers after the day's alienation
as prostitutes for a safety-valve for the family.

Womens liberation is impossible wi thout the destruction of the
class system - and a middle-class womens movement can't do
that. It's only the oppressed and exploited people who have
the strategic power to overthrow capitalism. We need an
organisation which recognises our particular oppression
and gives us a framework to meet in and work out a common
direction. The small groups that there are now must become
fighting units. We can't afford to be afraid to criticise each other-
the only real sisterhood is fighting side by side.....

The attack on Miss World was great - we need also to go
beneath it, beyond symbolic demonstrations to build a strong
supportive movement of women who will take the offensive.

WE'RE NOT
BEAUTIFUL
HE'RE NOT
UGLY.
HE'RE
ANGRY

The **Why Miss World** pamphlet was written, illustrated and printed after the trial of the Miss World protesters in 1971 by some of the women involved, including Sue Finch, Jenny Fortune, Jane Grant, Jo Robinson, and Sarah Wilson.

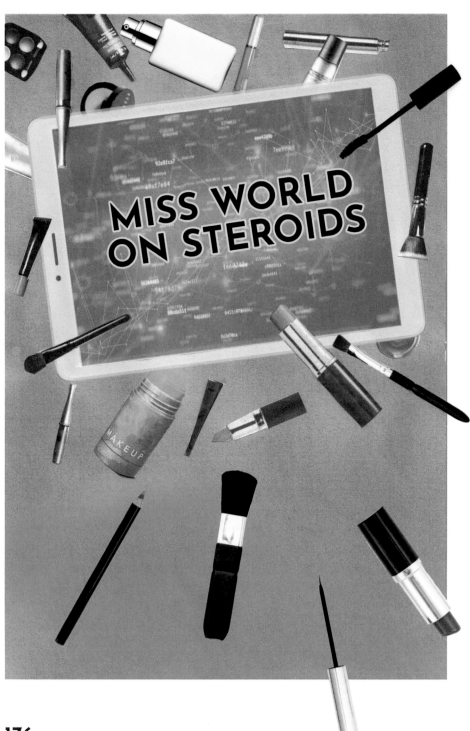

Miss World on steroids

FROM THE MISS WORLD DEMONSTRATION 1970
TO CAYLA THE DOLL AND PRETTY LITTLE THINGS 2020
BY JENNY FORTUNE

In 1970, after our success in halting the spectacle of the Miss World contest, we were surprised by the unexpected win of first and second place by two black women in what had always been a very white, conservative contest. Jennifer Hosten from Grenada and Pearl Jansen, the black woman transported in as Miss Africa South. This was Mecca's ruse to defuse the anti-apartheid campaigners' protests about apartheid South Africa being allowed to participate (Miss South Africa was white). The win gave rise to complex questions about the relationship between sex, race and class, which the Women's Liberation Movement was only just beginning to become awkwardly aware of.

In 2017, a talking doll named Cayla was banned by German authorities. The Federal Network Agency recommended that parents destroy the doll.

In 2020, Pretty Little Things, a clothes and accessories online warehouse in Sheffield made record profits during the Covid-19 pandemic.

What is the connection? This is a story that takes us from that anger-fuelled feminist action through the globalisation of the beauty industry to today's super-charged online sales and surveillance technology.

The winning of the 1970 competition by two black women foretold a period of extraordinary expansion of the tentacles of the beauty industry into the countries of the global south, which had hitherto had their very own specific ideas and practices in relation to female and male beauty. World-wide, beauty parlours, and barbers, were traditionally places to share tips about caring for black hair and skin, but importantly they were places of social gathering and information.

The 1960s 'Black is Beautiful' consciousness movement in America not only expressed black peoples' resistance to racism and colonialism across the world, it also celebrated black beauty as defined by black people, and the word was spread via these parlours. The Black Power movement enabled black women to realise their own power and strengthen their voices. Listening to these voices (Angela Davis, Audre Lorde, bell hooks amongst many others), we have learnt something about black women's consciousness – and beauty. At the same time so has the globalised beauty industry. As African American beauty manufacturers boomed, with a huge growth in demand for products that enhanced rather than erased black beauty, they soon began facing hostile competition from large non-black corporations. Revlon was the most aggressive in taking over that market, making free use of black manufacturers' products and brand symbols (*No Lye: An American Beauty Story*, Bayer Mack documentary, 2019). So grew the hold of the beauty industry, launched from the US into the global south.

The 1980s heralded the backlash against the power of the liberation and socialist movements of the 60s and 70s, ideologically framed by a new (but old) economic belief-system called 'monetarism' or 'neo-liberalism'. Underpinning this set of ideas was the belief in the so-called 'trickle-down effect', where wealth creation ('the trickle-up effect') would enable billionaires to invest their capital freely where and how they wanted, with no fear of restraint from democratic and national regulation. This would supposedly enrich local populations who had not been reached before by wealth creation. Oligarchs throughout the world licked their lips at the opportunities for self-enrichment and embraced the new philosophy. Freed from democratic restraints, western money markets were enabled to flood the global south with investment capitalism.

Beauty pageants and western-sponsored wars (most notably the Gulf wars and the ongoing 'War on Terror') embedded western finance, western culture, and western values, echoing Bob Hope's serving up of the Miss Worlds of 1969 and 1970 to the American troops in Vietnam. Western – American and European – cosmetics industries exploded into the beauty cultures of the south, led by the establishment of the beauty pageant as an exemplar of national pride. Beauty contests began entering the global south as a marker of sophistication and achievement from the 1990s onwards. In Africa, India, Asia and Latin America, young women began turning to beauty contests as a way out of acute poverty. Venezuela is globally ranked first in the number of beauty contests held there, and in the number of Miss World winners (*New York Times*, May 19, 2018). Young women's only way of affording the gowns, glitter and breast enhancements is to find a wealthy man:

> *I quickly learnt that getting into the Miss Venezuela contest meant I would have to prostitute myself.* (Abady, T. 'Pimping Out Miss Venezuela', New York Times, 19 May 2018)

A young Nigerian woman won Miss Universe 2001. Judges had picked a 'global beauty', which apparently included being thin. Susie Orbach in her book ' Bodies' illustrates the impact of the 'thinness':

> *As Ms Darego started to appear in magazines and billboards in Nigeria, she changed the aesthetic for young Nigerian women, who had first experienced her look as malnourished, but then went on to desire it for themselves. Inadvertently she instigated a dieting craze, a phenomenon that had not previously existed.* (Orbach, S. Bodies, Profile Books, London 2019)

In China the first ever beauty contest – Miss Artificial Beauty! – was held in 2003, a classic meeting of three obsessions in New China: beauty pageants, the western 'look' and plastic surgery.

'The winner, Qian Feng, said, "the nips and tucks were to enhance my beauty, but also to see what it was like, since I planned a career in the business." The operations gave her Western-style double eyelids and sculpted her face into its heart-shaped form, while liposuction made her thin'. (Coonan C. *China crowns first Miss Artificial Beauty*, The Irish Times, Dec.20. 2004)

Poorer Chinese girls who can't afford the 'western eyelid' plastic surgery have taken to creating sticky plasters to tape on their eyelids in order to duplicate the Western 'round' eye. (Orbach, S. 2019) By 2020 the Chinese cosmetics industry was the world's second largest market after the US. (Agnes Blyte, Statista.com accessed June 9th 2020)

In India, Sana Alam wrote in her blog:

> *In 1994, for the first time in the history of international beauty pageants, both Miss Universe and Miss World crowns adorned Indian heads. It was a moment of sheer appreciation and surprise because no-one could think of Indian girls to be the winners of both these titles since Western or Venezuelan women have always bagged these. And a nation that was just about getting a grip on itself in the post-globalised economy was suddenly shocked in awe. Indian beauties got a whole new face, and it empowered women. One example of the sudden entry of beauty brands has to be Revlon, the* **first ever international cosmetic brand** *to enter India. In the year 1995, due to a formidable coalition between the Modi Group and Revlon, it entered Indian markets as* **Modi Revlon**. (accessed 30 April 2020)

Revlon's global sales doubled to $3 billion between 2011 and 2017. (Statista.com, accessed 2 September 2020)

Here we see exposed the function of beauty pageants as a means of building the beauty industry's global markets and its intertwining with political power. The promotion of women's identity as the object of men's desire, and as a symbol of national identity has been used by expansionist projects for centuries (cf the Trojan Wars). This aspect of male power has now been stepped up to a super-industrial scale, with money to be made out of promoting and selling beauty products linked to political and financial power and networks.

'Modi-Mundipharma Beauty Products Pvt Ltd. is a name to reckon with in the beauty industry in India' says their advertising blurb. Although not directly linked, the name Modi carries weight because Narendra Modi is the Prime Minister of India and leader of the far-right BJP – the Hindu-led India People's Party. He rose to power on the back of the anti-Muslim pogrom in 2002 which led to over 1000 Muslims being killed in Gujarat. Since his election as Prime Minister of India in 2014, he has been conducting politics as an act of constant war against the Muslim population of India and Pakistan, stoking inter-racial, caste and religious violence. Politicians who win power like Modi need access to millions to fund and bribe their route to power nowadays – is the use of the name Modi coincidental?

Modi and Trump celebrated their 'special relationship' in India in February 2020 with a 'Namaste Trump' parade. Amidst the spectacle of many hugs and kisses between the two, Modi said,

> A special leader like President Trump and such a special friend coming to India is a big occasion' (Fuchs M. H. 'Trump and Modi', Guardian. 26 February 2020).

In the US, Donald Trump used his beauty pageant business (Miss Universe) to boost his international profile, in particular enabling a 'special relationship' with Russia.

The spread of beauty pageants globally opened up deep sores embedded by the racism of colonialism and slavery. Meetha Jha describes how:

...beauty has become a site of struggle over class, caste inequality, racism and respectability. The negative correlation of degrees of darkness of skin has been well documented. Skin colour, class, the body and beauty as a form of embodied capital. (Jha M. *The global beauty industry: Colorism, racism and the National Body,* Routledge 2015)

Beauty can provide access to higher income spouses, higher education and more financial security, simply put, a path to a better life, – but for some, not others. Recent global pageants in Asia and Africa have become sites for protest against Western domination. The 2002 riot in Nigeria, when 220 people died, was brought on by religious conflict in relation to the introduction of Sharia law. Those beauty protests dating from the 1960s 'Black is Beautiful' black-consciousness movement in the USA have spread into 'Dark is beautiful' and 'Brown 'n' Proud' in India, opening up awareness to the way the beauty industry appropriates, commodifies and markets women's bodies for the beauty industry. But whilst feminist awareness of the appropriation of our identities expanded globally, so did the reach of the cosmetics industry, with unprecedented global sales of $330 billion by 2011. (Jones, G. *Globalisation and Beauty,* Harvard University Press, EurAmerica Vol. 41. No.4. Dec 2011)

What is the vehicle that enables this extraordinary rate of expansion? Global media circuits, such as Instagram, Facebook, You Tube, Twitter and web blogs, are spreading norms and values that promote Western ideals of beauty – long straight hair, fair skin, round eyes, white even teeth, pert figures. The circuits maintain a global beauty industry devoted to skin lightening, skin bleaching creams, corrective cosmetic surgery, dieting and fashion. Unilever's skin lightener 'Fair & Lovely' was launched in forty countries in Asia, Africa, Caribbean and the Middle East from 1992 onwards. By 2017 Unilever's India market was worth $3 million annually.

But the cosmetics industry has to be supersensitive to trends in cultural movements, has to be careful not to strike a jarring, racist chord and remain at the forefront of 'what women want'. When black women rebelled against the oppressive hegemony of the thin white supermodel, cosmetic companies responded with the 'Brazilian butt', thanks to Beyoncé & Kim Kardashian. Beautiful big bums became officially approved as desirable and buyable commodities. By 2015 the 'Brazilian butt' was the most popular cosmetic enhancement globally at a cost of $10,000-$17,000 per operation. The African American grooming market is now worth $592 million a year. The industry has woken up fairly recently to the fact that black women in the US and Europe spend nearly nine times more than white women on their hair and beauty.

Acquiring deep knowledge about street culture has long been necessary to the fashion and beauty industries, as the very nature of the industry is based on the requisite to be a leader in fashion and THE cultural influencer. But the leaders of these industries are pale, male (or male oriented) and stale and haven't a hope in hell of being ahead of the mainstream because they ARE the mainstream. The industry has to turn to the street, where the real innovative culture is taking place. The very nature of being young and feeling you are an 'outsider' demands its own rebellious culture, and this was epitomised by the hip-hop movement of the 1970s. The Black Spades, influenced by the Black Panthers and the teaching of Malcolm X, took to the street with their own block parties, their own music and dance, their own 'look'. The cultural industries couldn't get over their excitement at this explosion of innovative imagination and began their inexorable appropriation of every aspect of this revolutionary culture – music, fashion, dance, the spirit of rebellion, celebration of difference. The beauty magazines' covers began to showcase the beauty of black people, to the point where *Teen Vogue* complains about the dominance of black women on magazine covers in 2018. (Rasool A. *Teen Vogue* 8 July 2018)

With its greed for expanding markets and the targeting of the black communities, what cosmetics companies are doing is promoting beauty products and sales as a way out of poverty (again) for both black and white women. Companies like That Sister offer black women the dream of setting up their own business. If black women spend so much on beauty products, what could go wrong? This is what can go wrong: my daughter's friend was persuaded to bulk buy cosmetics and beauty products from That Sister, wisely avoiding the usual contract which would have tied her in to buying their branded products at £150 a month for two years. She set up a rental contract for a corner shop near where she lives for two years. Full of plans and excitement she borrowed and spent a lot of money on doing up the shop and buying the merchandise. She wasn't given any marketing advice or support – not only did she not attract the black female clientele she anticipated, she did attract the attention of the two adjacent pubs which happened to be full of white racists. After six months of racist abuse and attacks she had to shut up shop and was left with a lot of beauty products and the rental for the remaining period.

This is not a new story; my generation may have had mothers who fell for the Elizabeth Arden (now a subsidiary of Revlon) pyramid schemes or became 'Avon Ladies'. The schemes were devised as a way of getting women who were stuck at home to sell cosmetics to each other, using coffee morning friendship circles and progressing to enlisting other women to do the same, until there were literally thousands of 'Avon Ladies'. Today, the Avon Lady is getting a digital makeover: CEO of Avon, Jan Zijdfeld says he wants Avon Ladies to become 'e-representatives', targeting contacts through Instagram, Twitter and Facebook. 'Friends selling to friends ... You trust your friends, the lady you may know.' (Gray A. 'Avon Lady gets a digital makeover', *Financial Times* 23 September 2018.) Pyramid schemes are now more commonly referred to as 'Multi-Level Marketing' (MLM) and have recently been exposed by Mumsnet: 'Mumsnet decided in 2017 not to allow MLMs to advertise on the parenting site. 'We thought about it long and hard because we know that home-based, flexible opportunities are very popular', says founder Justine Roberts, 'but many Mumsnet users have posted about what they see as MLMs' invidious marketing techniques and the effects on vulnerable individuals, and we came to the conclusion that business models based primarily on recruiting have too much potential to be exploitative.' (Tate A. *Multi-level beauty businesses, Guardian* June 1.2019)

The forces behind these coercive tactics have now found the Holy Grail of marketing – what is currently known as Surveillance Technology. At its most obvious level, this technology is simply the use of online social media to access and manipulate people's opinions and choices. We now know more about how deeply and powerfully manipulative the use of surveillance technology has become, thanks to *The Big Hack* and the investigative journalism of Carole Cadwalldr. (*Guardian*, February 2017) They exposed the scandal of Cambridge Analytica, a data collection enterprise developed to illegally shape voters' preferences in the US presidential election of 2016 and the Brexit referendum of 2016 in the UK (*Guardian*, 17 March 2018). Cambridge Analytica set up a pilot research project where a selected audience was paid to answer a survey. The personal data of up to eighty-seven million Facebook users were acquired via the 270,000 Facebook users who answered the survey and used the Facebook app called 'This Is Your Digital Life.' By giving this third-party app permission to acquire their data, back in 2015, this also gave the app access to information on the user's friends' networks; resulting in Cambridge Analytica illegally acquiring the data of about eighty seven million users. Cambridge Analytica was then paid by a US billionaire, Robert Mercer, and Aaron Banks, a millionaire British businessman supporter of Nigel Farage's Leave campaign, to access and influence British voters via Facebook and other online activities, to vote Leave in the referendum on European membership in 2016. Channel 4 news on 19 March 2018 further exposed how Cambridge Analytica was using whatever method available: data collection, psychological profiling and targeting of millions of voters, as well as more conventional blackmail and corruption.

And so the dots join up from Cambridge Analytica to Revlon. The beauty industry has found its dream machine in surveillance technology: access to the personal data of billions of internet users. The machinery of psychological profiling, targeting and manipulation is now being constructed on a global scale via data extraction that mines ever deeper into our personal lives. Global media networks are being used to shape human behaviour on a scale undreamt of before. The pinnacle of achievement for the advertising industry is to deliver predictable outcomes – predictable consumer purchasing and therefore profits. Global finance markets have long practised gambling on future sales and profits (Note 1). Predictable consumer profits are the golden chalice: reliable profits that can be used to bundle up and disguise the riskier gambles (Note 2).

In 2019 annual sales of the top five cosmetic brands amounted to $96 billion. (*Beauty Laid Bare*, BBC 3 documentary, 2 February 2020)

> *Today sees the release of the first comprehensive valuation of the British beauty industry and – in a revelation that will prove challenging to those who continue to dismiss it as the preserve of girls and gays – it turns out to make a bigger contribution to our economy than car manufacturing or publishing.* (Hannah Betts, *Telegraph*, 18 July 2019)

In the global economic slump that will certainly be generated by the coronavirus pandemic, the 'Lipstick Effect' will mean that the beauty industry is one of the few that will maintain its value. When people can't afford a more expensive luxury item, they will buy a cosmetic to give them a feeling of experiencing self-pampering, luxury and change. All this means that the invasive forces of data mining on women and on all young consumers – 20-24 year olds are the highest spenders on cosmetics (*Beauty Laid Bare*, 2020) – will be stepped up.

During the coronavirus lock down, one of the largest online distribution warehouses in the UK of beauty products and fashion, Pretty Little Things, was busier than during the Christmas period (*Sheffield Star*, 14 April 2020). Pretty Little Things is a distribution warehouse that specialises in online delivery of fashion and beauty products that sprang up in 2019 on the outskirts of Sheffield. It has taken over the site and buildings of what used to be one of the largest steel mills in the UK at Tinsley, Sheffield. What is happening in a once great industrial city exemplifies how the capitalist process of production is changing: from mining coal and ore for steel for armaments, to mining data for sales of beauty products.

Increasingly, the hardware that we rely on, and delight in – phones, tablets, personal computers – are gathering this deep data about our behaviour. When teenage girls confide in each other, or swap experiences, the data-gathering algorithms (Note 3) are sucking up every nuance to transform it into hard data, saleable to the cosmetics and fashion industries. You may say 'nothing new here, advertising companies have always done this', but this process is turbo-charged and is now an altogether different creature, invading our privacy at the deepest level.

Specialised cameras in our hardware analyse nano-second body language as we communicate: blinks, eye movement, smiles or shrugs.

> *Emotion analytics products such as SEWA use specialised software to scour faces, voices, gestures, bodies and brains, all of it captured by bio-metric and depth sensors, often in combination with imperceptibly small, unobtrusive cameras'* writes Shoshana Zuboff. (Zuboff, S. *The Age of Surveillance Capitalism*, Profile 1 June 2019)

> *Using facial recognition technology, your intentions, motives, meanings, needs, preferences, desires, emotions, personality and disposition are analysed.* (Zuboff, S.)

Zuboff explains how inner life becomes raw material to be extracted and worked on in a process of 'body rendition' – literally turning inner needs and insecurities into marketable products which will then render your outward appearance into the desired image. This process of body rendition is carried out by the consumer, turning herself into a marketable commodity which also consumes – the perfect circle! Millions are spent on cosmetics, clothes, slimming solutions, chemical enhancers (or lighteners), cosmetic surgery. As with Pretty Little Things, happiness becomes a service that can be delivered daily to your doorstep.

My Friend Cayla, the talking doll, was every little girl's dream, marketed at girls between 4-13 years, with her fair skin, blue eyes and blonde hair, she was the dream companion. She could listen and respond, able to receptively take in the little girl's hesitant confidences and sympathetically give advice. The only problem was that there was an adult listening and responding at the other end, via the doll's embedded speech recognition technology, which could be accessed from any mobile phone. The Germans, with their experience of the listening technologies employed by the Nazis and during the cold war, have enforceable privacy laws and banned the doll in 2017. The doll has also been criticised by the Norwegian Consumer Council for allowing the use of the collected data from the child's speech for targeted advertisements and other commercial purposes and its sharing with third parties, as well as for hidden advertisements through the doll's positive statements about certain products and services. (Tangen, G. B. *Cayla forbudt i Tyskland, på salg i Norge*, 2017. Accessed 11 November 2017.)

Deep data collection and transmission to be used in the shaping and directing of female identities is being targeted at girls from infancy. The feminism of the 1970s revealed the shaping of female identities from childhood into a constrictive gender formula. Embodied by the 39-25-36 vital statistic insisted on as a measure of female beauty, feminists first demonstrated against the intrusion of beauty contests into our identities at the Miss World contest of 1970. Little would we have dreamt of the technologies of penetration and manipulation that global beauty markets would subsequently develop. Our generation has a strong resistance against the incursions of surveillance technology in undermining and appropriating our self-esteem, and of course, that sense of 'the male gaze'. We did not grow up with the delights and dangers of online media communication, and so are relatively unbothered by online manipulation and the drive to consumerism. New generations of feminists are skilled in using the technological tools, but the tools are still predominantly designed by men for a male-defined world. Google (Nelson, A. 'Google and the Structural Sexism of the American Workplace', Forbes. 30.10.2018), Facebook (O'Toole E. 'Facebook's Violently Sexist Ads', Guardian 23 May 2013), and Apple are notorious as companies that are imbued with sexism (Mahdawi, A. 'Apple's Sexist Credit Card', Guardian, 13 November 2019) and now we all know what happens with Cambridge Analytica.

Maybe one of the most powerful antidotes we have to this deep manipulation is the joy and excitement we discover in expressing our anger together. As we did with bringing the beauty contest to a halt in 1970, younger women are again experiencing that joy and power in deciding for themselves, together, what their lives are going to be like. We are going to freely enjoy the beauty of our own and each other's bodies without 'THE MAN MAKING MONEY OUT OF US'.

L to R: **Alexa Davies** (plays Sue), **Sue Finch, Jenny Fortune, Jane Grant, Sarah Wilson, Ruby Benthall** (plays Sarah)**, Jo Robinson and Kate McClean at the premier of** *Misbehaviour***.** Photo courtesy of Pathé

Reverberations of Misbehaving in Radio, Television and Film

Stories from some of the people who created radio and television documentaries along with the feature film, *Misbehaviour*, inspired by the Miss World 1970 protest

Actors Keira Knightley (Sally) and Jessie Buckley (Jo) running away from a freshly painted billboard in **Misbehaviour**. Still from Misbehaviour provided courtesy of Pathé.

Grafitti by two women on a billboard opposite their office at the **Morning Star**
© Jill Posener, 1979 Farringdon Road, London

Sue MacGregor WAS BORN IN OXFORD AND GREW UP IN CAPE TOWN. FROM AN EARLY AGE SHE DREAMED OF WORKING IN RADIO, WHICH WAS JUST AS WELL, AS THERE WAS NO TV IN SOUTH AFRICA UNTIL 1976. SHE MOVED BACK TO THE UK AND ACHIEVED HER DREAM, THANKS TO BBC RADIO 4, STARTING AS A REPORTER ON THE **WORLD AT ONE**, MOVING ON TO PRESENT **WOMAN'S HOUR**, **TODAY**, AND THEN **THE REUNION**. IN 2020 SHE CELEBRATED OVER FIFTY YEARS ON BBC RADIO.

Thoughts on making a Reunion about the Miss World contest 1970

I always thought of myself as particularly lucky to be the voice, if you like, of *The Reunion*, which I was for about seventeen years, because in my experience most of the hard work in documentary programmes is done by a researcher, who is generally a clued-up woman on a freelance contract, prepared to spend several weeks finding exactly the right people to invite into the studio to talk about an event that happened years before. Without the relentless delving of a researcher, and the approval and help of the editor of *The Reunion's* inventor David Prest, the programmes simply wouldn't take off.

That being said, the presenter of any programme needs to know her stuff. So mindful of this, I pulled an ancient BBC diary off the shelf in my study to see if on the 20th November 1970, I had marked up the Miss World competition as worth watching on the telly. There was no mention of it at all. But I kicked myself for not watching it, or for not even being there in the Royal Albert Hall, for in many ways this was a significant early indication of how determined the women in the Women's Movement in the UK were to show their contempt for beauty contests and all that they meant. There were other reasons for regretting not watching live: Bob Hope, still well known in 1970, was the official compere who rather lost the plot after the well-primed women protesters in the audience hurled their flour bags at the stage; Hope that evening made some nasty public accusations against anyone who could dream of interrupting a beauty contest. Another reason to be there was that South Africa was allowed to field two contestants: one called Miss South Africa (she was white) and the other Miss Africa South (a woman of colour). We were still very much in the age of apartheid in South Africa, and this was a very controversial decision all round. In the end Miss Africa South was not quite the winner but came close as the runner up. The winner was Jennifer Hosten, Miss Grenada, who went on to be, among other things, a successful diplomat.

Thanks to the excellent researcher, the *Reunion* programme we made in 2010 included some of the most important figures of the event back in 1970: Jennifer Hosten herself, the first woman of colour to wear the Miss World crown; Peter Jolley representing the Mecca organisation which then ran the Miss World competition in the UK; Michael Aspel who compered the original show, and three of the flour bombers – Jo Robinson, Sally Alexander and Jenny Fortune.

Roll forward ten years to the 9th March 2020, and an invitation came from the makers of a new film to the premiere of *Misbehaviour* which had a starry cast including Keira Knightley, Keeley Hawes and Lesley Manville. It was very much based on what happened in the Royal Albert Hall back in August 1970 – and was fairly light-hearted in tone. All the performances were good, and they needed to be, as a portion of the film company's guests in the cinema that night were the real people who had been on stage that memorable night, including Jennifer Hosten, the winner, and Miss Africa South, Pearl Jansen. They all looked as if they were pleased to be there … and yet I knew a few of them had reservations, which I shared. For anyone who had actually lived in South Africa in the 60s and 70s, whether they were white or, as the government there then called those not white, Non-European, there wasn't quite enough in the movie to explain just how extraordinary it was that a

South African woman of colour had come second in an international glamour competition, and that she was only just beaten for the crown by another woman of colour, from Grenada in the Caribbean.

Fifty years on from Miss World 1970, Beauty Pageants are still highly popular in a huge number of countries. The Big Four are still Miss World, Miss Universe, Miss International and Miss Earth, though the Miss World competition finally disappeared from our television screens here in Britain in 1988.

Hannah Berryman
SPECIALISES IN TELLING CONTEMPORARY HISTORICAL STORIES WITH BROADER CULTURAL RESONANCE, INCLUDING THE BBC2 DOCUMENTARY **MISS WORLD: BEAUTY QUEENS & BEDLAM** WHICH LOOKED AT THE FEMINIST PROTEST AND SOCIAL AND POLITICAL STRUGGLES SURROUNDING THE 1970 MISS WORLD CONTEST. SHE ALSO MADE THE SUCCESSFUL GRIERSON-SHORTLISTED SERIES **PRINCESS MARGARET: THE REBEL ROYAL**, GRIERSON-NOMINATED **HIGH SOCIETY BRIDES**, AND GRIERSON-SHORTLISTED **A VERY ENGLISH EDUCATION**, AS WELL AS **ROCKFIELD: THE STUDIO ON THE FARM.**

I was keen to make a documentary about the historic 1970 Miss World protest because it seemed a great way to tell the bigger story of the birth of the modern feminist movement here in the UK, a story that would not have been possible to tell on mainstream terrestrial TV without it. I wanted women (and men) of today to be able to discover just how bad things were for women at that time, and the important work which started to change things in that year.

I knew that in 1970 the Women's Liberation Movement had held their first ever conference, and that it was brilliantly filmed for a documentary from the time: *A Woman's Place*. All my films rely on archive as well as interviews, so I looked into what else there was and discovered a BBC documentary from the time 'People For Tomorrow', where there were lots of filmed interviews with women from the original women's movement. In addition, *Man Alive* had made a film following the Miss World contest a couple of years earlier, and there was other intriguing film footage from the 1970 contest, with the first ever black winner, Jennifer Hosten, and the first ever non-white South African contestant, Pearl Jansen. I could see there was a rich tale to tell. As research went on I knew that just as important as the story of the women's movement would be these stories of the women of colour in the contest.

Although there was a feature film being made too, I knew that this focused more on the event itself, and that through finding the original protestors and contestants, I could contextualise it, and bring home more broadly the sexism and racism of life in 1970, so that viewers could understand the importance of the changes from that year. Animation is often a feature of my work, used to fill in the gaps of the archive and get a sense of the feel of the times. I knew we could use it to bring to life the planning of the protest and how it must have felt back then – just what was involved in bringing such a major event to a standstill.

The women interviewed, both protestors and contestants, were without exception superb and enlightening on that year itself and the wider struggles they were wrestling with. I'm proud to have had the opportunity to make this documentary.

Rebecca Frayn IS A NOVELIST, SCREENWRITER/FILM MAKER AND ENVIRONMENTAL ACTIVIST. MANY OF HER PROJECTS HAVE CHAMPIONED WOMEN'S STORIES INCLUDING **THE LADY**, THE SCREENPLAY SHE ORIGINATED AND WROTE ABOUT AUNG SAN SUU KYI, DIRECTED BY LUC BESSON, WHICH WAS AWARDED THE INTERNATIONAL HUMAN RIGHTS FILM AWARD IN 2012. **MISBEHAVIOUR** WAS CO-ORIGINATED WITH THE PRODUCER SUZANNE MACKIE AND WRITTEN BY REBECCA.

Misbehaviour was a decade long passion project for Suzanne Mackie the producer and me. For ten long years we both kept the flame burning through an extraordinary number of drafts and an extraordinary number of setbacks. Our mutual obsession began when, sitting in different parts of London, we both just happened to hear the same documentary on Radio 4 that charted the moment when women disrupted the Miss World show and in doing so undertook the first direct action since the Suffragettes. We met in a state of great excitement a few days later to agree that here was a story just crying out to be told as a feature film. It was a story that had mischief and humour, with a message so incredibly relevant to the modern world that women everywhere needed to know it!

But in 2010, after the undoubted progress of the '70s, feminism was in a long state of stagnation and so despite our enthusiasm, financiers showed at best tepid interest. Whilst they might pay lip service to the importance of gender issues, you could see only too clearly the dead look behind their eyes. Fortunately, Natasha Wharton at the British Film Institute (BFI) stepped in and agreed to fund two drafts – and at last we were off!

Cut to a new setback when source material soon proved tricky to locate and draft after draft failed to convince the BFI that we had a story that would work. And all the while the years were passing. Sometimes my husband Andy, a television producer, would find me slumped in despair over my desk, battling yet again with a whole new radical approach. And being the loving husband he is, his advice was always the same, 'It's never going to work, darling. Best to just face the fact you're wasting your time and move on.' And then with a slam of the door he would be gone, off to sort out more pressing problems in the world.

Yet neither Suzanne nor I could shake the conviction that if only we could unlock it, this was a story that could work on the big screen. And it was only after the BFI eventually gave up on me, that I finally saw a way of doing it and wrote a speculative draft that the BFI decided to back again, that Philippa Lowthorpe the director signed on for and Pathe then bought. Amazingly, only a few months later in 2017, the thunderclap of the Women's marches and Me Too took the world by storm and our marginal story was suddenly – miraculously – very much part of the zeitgeist.

We owe an incalculable debt to all those remarkable women who helped found the Women's Movement in Oxford at the beginning of 1970 and all those hundreds more who took part in all kinds of activism to help launch a new social movement that was to transform women's lives for the better. As Margaret Mead the American cultural anthropologist so cogently phrased it,

'Never doubt that a small group of thoughtful, committed citizens can change the world; indeed, it's the only thing that ever has'.

Suzanne Mackie

HAS WORKED IN THE FILM AND TELEVISION INDUSTRY FOR OVER TWENTY-FIVE YEARS, ORIGINATING AND PRODUCING FEATURE FILMS **CALENDAR GIRLS, KINKY BOOTS** FOR BUENA VISTA AND **MISBEHAVIOUR** FOR PATHE SINCE 2013 SUZANNE HAS BEEN EXECUTIVE PRODUCER OF MULTI-AWARD WINNING **THE CROWN** FOR NETFLIX. SHE WAS CREATIVE DIRECTOR AT AWARD WINNING LEFT BANK PICTURES WHERE SHE EXECUTIVE PRODUCED THE HIT SERIES **MAD DOGS** FOR SKY ONE, BAFTA WINNING **THE REPLACEMENT** FOR BBC 1 AND SIX-PART DRAMA **BEHIND HER EYES** FOR NETFLIX.

The idea for the film *Misbehaviour* was precipitated by the brilliant Radio 4 *Reunion* programme, which brought together the protagonists of the 1970s Miss World event some forty years later.

I was heading out to work, with half of my attention on the radio show. But what I heard made me stop in my tracks. I heard Sally Alexander, Jo Robinson and Jenny Fortune recount the event from the perspective of the women's liberation protest and I heard Jennifer Hosten recount her memories of being the 1970s winner of the Miss World crown, the first woman of colour to win the title and Michael Aspel, as host of the competition that year, share his perspective and memories. It was a lively discussion; a passionate one. Full of laughter and joy and with enough polite squabbling to make the reunion of these people, from all corners of the world, and from all sides of the political debate, a rather compulsive listen.

I found myself laughing and whooping, but I also found the true story immensely moving too.

As I listened two things occurred to me: that I had never heard about the story of the women's liberation demonstrations at the Miss World competition; and that this story should be made into a film!

As a producer I guess I have quite a good antenna for stories which might lend themselves to being dramatised. Like *Calendar Girls* and *Kinky Boots*, which were stories I helped nurture to the screen, my response to the Miss World story was very similar: that this was a human story about endeavour and passion; a bringing together of people from all walks of life who were prepared to do something that would make a difference and that could affect change. This 1970s event represents a moment in time that captures something moving, inspiring and courageous in the human spirit. These are stories that I love; that I respond to: stories that make me feel alive.

I rushed out to work (now late) full of a deep conviction that this story should be brought to the big screen.

I quickly tracked down Sally Alexander and Jo Robinson and soon after Jennifer Hosten in Canada, and having had an initial meeting with Sally at her beautiful house in Pimlico, I joined forces with screen writer Rebecca Frayn, who had also heard the radio programme and who'd had a similarly passionate response to the story.

Rebecca and I met up with Sally and Jo again and, convinced of the enormous potential of the story, we set forth on the long and complex journey of turning the wonderful true story into a feature film.

Films notoriously take a long time to develop and to achieve financial support. They can be something of a labour of love.

Misbehaviour was no exception. It ended up taking nearly ten years to be finally brought to the screen. Although our confidence in the idea never diminished, it was a story that, in many ways, needed to find its moment.

The British Film Institute had initially funded the development of the script, but then a couple of years ago Pathe approached us and said they were interested in making the film. And when soon after BBC Films also came on board, we knew the film finally had a chance to be made. Pathe had responded to a particular mood – a zeitgeist – in the country to which *Misbehaviour* was perfectly attuned.

Misbehaviour had found its moment.

It was at this point director Philippa Lowthorpe came on board, and, along with an excellently crafted screenplay, which elegantly wove together the many multifaceted story perspectives, Philippa's talent and reputation as a director meant we were able to attract a high calibre of cast and thus finally achieve a green light to make the film.

Getting to know the real women involved in this story, Jo and Sally, Sue, Sarah, Jane, Jenny from the original women's movement has been such a joy and an inspiration, as well as getting to know Jennifer Hosten and Pearl Jansen, who was the 1970s runner up, who we eventually tracked down in South Africa.

And one of the proudest moments in my career came at *Misbehaviour's* film premiere in London in early March 2020, when we filmmakers and actors stood on the stage, and joined arms together with these extraordinary women who had achieved so much, who also joined hands with the Miss World contestants.

Suddenly we were one; one group of passionate and strong women joined together to celebrate the film. And, in a post TimesUp atmosphere, to perhaps be part of a moment

It had taken ten long years to get to this place. Who could have known that only a week later when the film was released, Coronavirus was going to force closure of all cinemas across the land...

But perhaps that's not 'times up' for *Misbehaviour* and it's certainly not times up for these women!

Philippa Lowthorpe IS AN AWARD-WINNING FILM AND TELEVISION DIRECTOR. SHE IS THE FIRST, AND SADLY STILL THE ONLY WOMAN TO HAVE WON A BAFTA FOR BEST DIRECTOR FICTION IN THE BAFTA CRAFT AWARDS. SHE HAS ALSO BEEN AWARDED THE DIRECTOR AWARD AT THE WFTV FILM AND TELEVISION AWARDS FOR THE MINISERIES **THREE GIRLS**, WHICH WENT ON TO WIN FIVE BAFTAS IN 2018, INCLUDING A SECOND DIRECTING BAFTA FOR PHILIPPA. AS WELL AS THE FILM **MISBEHAVIOUR**, OTHER CREDITS INCLUDE **THE CROWN**, **CALL THE MIDWIFE** AND **THE THIRD DAY**

When I started out as a researcher in documentaries at Yorkshire TV, my first job after university in the late 1980s, there were no women directors. In fact, you weren't allowed to become a director without a union ticket. It really was a closed shop. In our department, there was a male boss who got round the situation by enabling a couple of women to make short items for our programme, *Where There's Life*, calling themselves 'producers'. When I look back now, I realise I was lucky to be in his department and see women older than me making these short films, and also going on to run the whole show, in the case of Gwyn Hughes, now an award-winning screen writer.

There are still not enough female directors, or directors from diverse backgrounds. The BFI keeps statistics on who has done what in the film industry. Since 1930, 94.5% of all films have been directed by men. I think it's been much harder for women to be trusted by bosses to handle positions of authority. We just don't look like what

Alexa Davies, Lily Newmark, Ruby Benthall, Jessie Buckley and Keira Knightley in *Misbehaviour*
© Pathé UK

people think a director should look like! When I was directing *The Crown*, I was quite often mistaken for an extra who had wandered into the wrong place, or someone from the costume department.

I know I have been disregarded as a potential director for a project because I am a woman, but I have also had people who believe in me too – both men and women. Having champions and supporters is vital if you're in a minority.

When I won my first BAFTA for TV drama directing, I hoped that, like the majority of male nominees and winners who'd won before me, I might be offered a film. Cinema was always my first love and I wanted to make something for the big screen. I was wrong. I noticed that while the chaps had got new opportunities, recognition and trust, I did not. I was the first woman to win this award and still the only one, which makes me disappointed and angry. Only a handful of women directors have even been nominated!

Five years later in 2018, when I won my second BAFTA for directing the BBC miniseries *Three Girls*, I had already been invited to be part of *Misbehaviour*, so things must have shifted a bit.   I think the #MeToo, Times Up and 50:50 movements have helped highlight inequalities in the film and TV industry. The industry is trying to change, but there is still a long way to go.

This is the reason I jumped at the chance of directing *Misbehaviour*. It's a hugely important story to tell and also speaks to issues close to my heart and my own experience of sexism and prejudice. The young feminists in the filmwho were part of the early Women's Liberation Movement were fighting for equality. They are brilliant role models and an inspiration to younger generations of women, and I wanted to help tell their story.

Keira Knightley and Director Philippa Lowthorpe on set of **Misbehaviour** © Pathe UK

Mary Higgins, Isis Hainsworth, Keira Knightley, Jessie Buckley and Ria Zmitrovicz, in *Misbehaviour* outside the court at the end of the trial. © Pathé UK

Acknowledgments

Many thanks to Sally Fraser for her wonderful photos of the Women's Liberation Conference and Movement 1970-1971, and to Liberation Films for permission to use stills from *A Woman's Place* 1971, a documentary about the Women's Liberation Conference, 1970 and the Women's Liberation march 1971.

We are very grateful to Ruthie Petrie for volunteering her invaluable support in editing *Misbehaving* – although any mistakes that remain are ours.

We are really grateful to Rebecca Frayn, Suzanne Mackie, and Philippa Lowthorpe for their persistence in making the film *Misbehaviour*, and, together with Sue MacGregor's *Reunion* radio programme and Hannah Berryman's BBC2 *Miss Word: Beauty Queens and Bedlam* documentary getting the story of the protest against Miss World 1970 out to a wider audience.

Thank you to Bea Campbell for bearing with us through the early stages of labour. Thanks also to Peter Dukes, Sam Lord, Jo Robinson and Sarah Wilson of Poster Workshop for permission to reproduce posters, and to Juliet Mitchell and Sheila Rowbotham for allowing us to reproduce photos they were in.

So many people encouraged and supported us that it would take up half the book to mention them all, but we would like especially to thank Pete Ayrton for publishing advice, and Mikela Panzeri, Morgan Stetler and Tony Swash for helping with preparation of the visual material for the book. Thank you to David Hoffman for permission to use his photo and to Chris Ratcliffe, of Pennine Pens, for his patient and ever helpful advice. Thanks to Nathan Ryder of Ryder Design for his initial design work and helpful advice.

We have made every effort to find copyright holders but were unsuccessful in locating Keith Bailey whose photograph of the Flashing Nipple show is, as far as we know, the only visual record of the actual event.

Alicia Kirkbride and Louise Halliday kindly opened the Royal Albert Hall Archives for us. Minna Haukka, artist/curator at the Feminist Library, found original artwork that we needed.

Thank you to Caroline Poland who shared her experience and expertise in publishing *You Can't Kill the Spirit, Houghton Main Pit Camp, South Yorkshire: the untold story of the women who set up camp to stop pit closure* – a wonderful book about Women Against Pit Closures. The exuberant spirit of the book inspired us to keep going with Misbehaving.

We would also like to thank Karen Taylor, who completed her Master of Arts Twentieth-Century Historical Studies degree on *Images of Feminism: A review of the Women's Liberation Movement's use of Propaganda by Deed at the Miss World demonstration on 20 November 1970 and at the subsequent trial of five of the protesters* (unpublished) in 1994, for researching the contemporary press coverage and sharing it with us.

Finally, endless thanks to our wonderful designer, Morgan Stetler.

References and Resources

BOOKS AND JOURNALS

Abady, T 'Pimping Out Miss Venezuela', *New York Times* 19 May 2018. Quoted in *Straight Walk* by P. Velazquez, Simon and Schuster 2015

Gay, R. 'Fifty Years Ago, Protesters Took on the Miss America Pageant and Electrified the Feminist Movement', *Smithsonian Magazine*, 2018 www.smithsonianmag.com/history/fifty-years-ago-protestors-took-on-miss-america-pageant-electrified-feminist-movement-180967504/ (Accessed 30 August 2020)

Jha, M. 'The global beauty industry: Colorism, racism and the National Body', *Routledge* 2015

Jones, G. 'Globalisation and Beauty: A Historical and Firm Perspective', *Ou Mei yan jui, [EurAmerica]* Vol.41 No.4. December 2011

Morgan, R 1968 'Robin Morgan papers', Duke University, in *Morris and Withers* 2018 *The Feminist Revolution, the struggle for women's liberation 1966-1988*, London: Virago

Morgan, R. 1970 'Goodbye to all That' blog.fair-use.org/2007/09/29/goodbye-to-all-that-by-robin-morgan-1970/ (accessed 30 August 2020)

Nelson, A. 'Google and the structural sexism of the American Workplace', *Forbes* 30 October 2018

Orbach, S. *Bodies*, Profile Books, London 2019

O'Sullivan 'Passionate Beginnings: Ideological Politics 1969-72', *Feminist Review* No. 11, 1982

Sheffield Women Against Pit Closures 'You Can't Kill the Spirit—Houghton Main Pit Camp, South Yorkshire: the untold story of the women who set up camp to stop pit closure' can be ordered by writing to SWAPC, c/o 6 Burnside Avenue Sheffield S8 9FR or emailing SWAPCPitCamp1993@gmail.com

Tangen, G. B. 'Cayla forbudt i Tyskland, på salg i Norge'. 2017 Accessed 11 November 2017

Zuboff S The Age of Surveillance Capitalism, Profile 2019

FILMS, RADIO, AND TELEVISION

A Woman's Place, film directed, scripted and produced by Sue Crockford, Ellen Adams and Tony Wickert; narrated by Sheila Adams, 1971. Held in the London Community Video Archive, www.the-lcva.co.uk, and in the archive of the British Film Institute. View for free: youtu.be/SlJ5IO7QbLU

Beauty Laid Bare, BBC 3 documentary, 2 February 2020

Misbehaviour, Philippa Lowthorpe (Director) Pathe 2020 The film is widely available for streaming online, and on DVD.

Miss World 1970: Feminists and Flour Bombs, Philippa Walker (Director) 2002 www2.bfi.org.uk/films-tv-people/4ce2b87782d9e

Miss World 1970: Beauty Queens and Bedlam, Hannah Berryman (Director), BBC 2, 2020 www.bbc.co.uk/iplayer/episode/m000gghb/miss-world-1970-beauty-queens-and-bedlam

No Lye: An American Beauty Story, Bayer Mack documentary released 5 May 2019

The Big Hack, documentary, 2018

The Reunion: Miss World 1970, Radio 4, Sue MacGregor (Presenter), 2010 www.bbc.co.uk/programmes/b00tkpc1

PHOTOGRAPHY

Fraser, S. search 'Sally Fraser' at www.reportdigital.co.uk

Hoffman, D. www.hoffmanphotos.com

ORGANISATIONS

The Feminist Library www.feministlibrary.co.uk
@FeministLibrary Facebook and Twitter
The Sojourner Truth Community Centre,
161 Sumner Rd, Peckham, London SE15 6JL

Poster Workshop www.posterworkshop.co.uk